SPOTLIGHT

SO-ARK-604

NEW BRUNSWICK

ANDREW HEMPSTEAD

Contents

Saint John and the Fundy Coast.......8

Planning Your Time...............11

Saint John and Vicinity 11

History...........................11
Liverpool of America...............13
World War II and Beyond............13

Getting Oriented 13

Sights...........................14
Downtown 14
◖ Prince William and
  Germain Streets.................15
West of Downtown 17

Recreation 18
Parks 18
◖ Irving Nature Park...............18
Water Sports.....................19

Entertainment and Events 19
Performing Arts 19
Pubs and Nightclubs..............19
Festivals and Events..............20

Shopping........................20

**Accommodations
  and Camping**..................20

Food............................22

Information and Services........23
Tourist Information 23
Books and Bookstores.............23
Post Office.......................23
Internet Services 23
Emergency Services...............23

Getting There 24

Air...............................24
Bus 24
Ferry.............................24

Getting Around..................24
Bus 24
Taxi..............................24

Saint John to St. Andrews.......24
Point Lepreau and Vicinity 24
St. George 25

St. Andrews and Vicinity....25
History...........................26

Sights...........................26
Historic Downtown...............27
◖ Kingsbrae Garden..............27
St. Andrews Blockhouse National
  Historic Site....................27
◖ Minister's Island Historic Site.....28
Huntsman Aquarium 28
Atlantic Salmon Interpretive Centre ..28

Shopping........................28

Recreation 28
On the Water.....................28
Golf.............................29

**Accommodations
  and Camping**..................29

Food............................ 31

Information 31

Fundy Isles 32

Deer Island......................32
Sights and Recreation 32
Accommodations 32
Getting There 32

Campobello Island...............32
  Parks 32
  Getting There 32
■ Grand Manan Island 33
  Bird-Watching 33
  Tours...........................33
  Accommodations and Camping 33
  Food 34
  Getting There 34

Upper Fundy Coast..........34
Saint John to Fundy
  National Park..............34
  St. Martins.....................34
■ Fundy National Park..........35
  Park Entry......................36
  Hiking..........................36
  Other Recreation 36
  Accommodations 36
  Campgrounds 36
  Food 37
  Information 37
Alma to Hopewell Cape 37
  Shepody National Wildlife Area 37
Hopewell Cape...................38
■ Hopewell Rocks 38
  Accommodations and Food.........39

Saint John
River Valley.............40
Planning Your Time..............40
Fredericton and Vicinity.........42
History.........................43
  The Capital's Fortuitous
    Beginning 43
  Expansion 44
  Fires and Floods.................44
  The Town Evolves................44

Sights..........................45
■ Historic Garrison District 45
  City Hall........................46
  Fredericton Lighthouse............46
■ Beaverbrook Art Gallery 47
  Legislative Assembly Building 47
■ Christ Church Cathedral 47
  Historic Cemeteries 47
  Odell Park 48
Recreation 48
Entertainment and Events 48
  Performing Arts 48
  Pubs and Nightlife 49
  Festivals and Events..............49
Shopping.......................49
  Arts and Crafts...................49
Accommodations
  and Camping..................49
Food...........................51
Information and Services........52
  Tourist Information 52
  Books and Bookstores.............52
  Services.........................52
Getting There 52
Getting Around..................53
Gagetown and Vicinity 53

Up the Saint John River.....53
Mactaquac and Vicinity 53
  Mactaquac Provincial Park 54
■ Kings Landing Historical
  Settlement 54
To Grand Falls 55
  Woodstock.......................55
■ Hartland Covered Bridge 55
  Grand Falls (Grand-Sault) 55
Edmundston and Vicinity........55
  Sights and Recreation 55

Accommodations 56
Saint-Jacques 56
Lac-Baker. 56

**Mount Carleton
    Provincial Park.** 56

Acadian Coast 57

Planning Your Time. 58

Moncton 60

Downtown Sights. 61
    ⟨ Bore Park. 61
    Moncton Museum 61
    Thomas Williams Heritage House 62
    Galerie d'Art et Musée Acadien 62

⟨ Magnetic Hill 63
    Commercial Attractions. 63

Recreation 64
    Centennial Park. 64
    Fun Parks. 64

Entertainment and Events 64
    Theater. 64
    Bars and Nightclubs. 64
    Festivals and Events. 64

Shopping 64

**Accommodations
    and Camping** 65

Food. 66

Information and Services. 67
    Tourist Information 67
    Books and Bookstores. 67
    Services 67

Getting There 67
    Air. 67
    Train and Bus 67

Getting Around. 67

Southeast from
Moncton .68

Memramcook. 68

Sackville 68
    ⟨ Sackville Waterfowl Park 68
    Accommodations and Food 68

Sackville to Aulac 69

Aulac and Vicinity. 69
    Fort Beauséjour 69
    Tintamarre Sanctuary. 69

Strait Coast 70

Cape Tormentine to Shediac. 70
    Cape Jourimain Nature Centre. 70
    Continuing West 70

Shediac 70
    ⟨ Parlee Beach 70
    Accommodations and Camping 70
    Food 71

Boutouche 71
    ⟨ Le Pays de la Sagouine 71
    Irving Eco-Centre 72

Kouchibouguac National Park 72
    Park Entry 72
    Recreation. 73
    Camping. 73
    Information 73

Miramichi River 73

Miramichi 73
    Sights. 74
    Festivals and Events. 75
    Accommodations and Camping 75
    Food 75
    Information 75

Miramichi to Fredericton 76
    Doaktown. 76
    Boiestown 76

Baie des Chaleurs 76

Acadian Peninsula. 76
  Bartibog Bridge 76
  Val-Comeau Provincial Park 76
  Shippagan 77

Île Lamèque 77
  [C] Lamèque International
    Baroque Music Festival 77
  Accommodations and Camping 78

Caraquet 78

Sights and Recreation 78
  [C] Village Historique Acadien........78
  Festivals and Events................78
  Accommodations and Food..........78

Grande-Anse 78

Bathurst and Vicinity 79
  Bathurst to Campbellton............79

Campbellton. 79
  Sights and Recreation 79
  Accommodations and Food 80

NEW BRUNSWICK

SAINT JOHN AND THE FUNDY COAST

Imagine the scene: A pervasive unearthly stillness. Seabirds wheel and dart across the horizon. Suddenly, the birds cry out in a chorus as the incoming tide approaches. The tidal surge, which began halfway around the world, in the southern Indian Ocean, quietly and relentlessly pours into the Fundy's mouth, creating the highest tides on the planet. Fishing boats are lifted from the muddy sea floor, and whales in pursuit of silvery herring hurry along the summertime currents, their mammoth hulks buoyed by the 100 billion tons of seawater that gush into the long bay between New Brunswick and Nova Scotia.

The cycle from low to high tide takes a mere six hours. The tide peaks, in places high enough to swamp a four-story building, and then begins to retreat. As the sea level drops,

coastal peninsulas and rocky islets emerge from the froth, veiled in seaweed. The sea floor reappears, shiny as shellac and littered with sea urchins, periwinkles, and shells. Where no one walked just hours ago, local children run and skip on the beaches, pausing to retrieve tidal treasures. New Brunswickers take the Fundy tides for granted. For visitors, it's an astounding show.

The Fundy Coast is a paradox: It's at once the most- and least-developed part of the province. Saint John—the province's largest city and major port—sits at the midpoint. To either side, the coastline is remotely settled and wonderfully wild. The region is best considered as two distinct areas, with Saint John interposed between them. The Lower Fundy, situated at the bay's southwestern end, includes

© ANDREW HEMPSTEAD

HIGHLIGHTS

◖ Prince William and Germain Streets: Downtown Saint John oozes history at every corner, but nowhere is it as concentrated as along these two streets (page 15).

◖ Irving Nature Park: Nature is left to its own devices within this oceanfront park, but what makes it remarkable is its vicinity to a major shipping port (page 18).

◖ Kingsbrae Garden: Blending formal gardens with trails through Acadian coastal forest, Kingsbrae will soothe your senses (page 27).

◖ Minister's Island Historic Site: Yes, wandering through the 50-room summer home of a railway magnate is interesting, but getting there along a road exposed only at low tide is half the fun (page 28).

◖ Grand Manan Island: Bird-watchers will want to catch the ferry over to this Bay of Fundy island to watch the abundance of seabirds that gather each spring and fall (page 33).

◖ Fundy National Park: Protecting a huge swath of Fundy coastline, this park offers plenty of chances to get back to nature or, if you prefer, the opportunity to go golfing and feast on fresh seafood (page 35).

◖ Hopewell Rocks: This attraction, where you can "walk on the ocean floor," is a wonderful natural phenomenon helped along by the massive Fundy tides – just don't expect to find solitude (page 38).

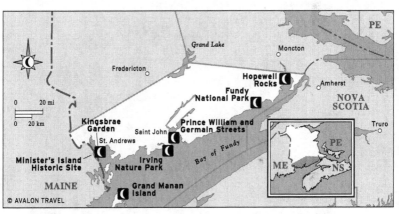

LOOK FOR ◖ TO FIND RECOMMENDED SIGHTS, ACTIVITIES, DINING, AND LODGING.

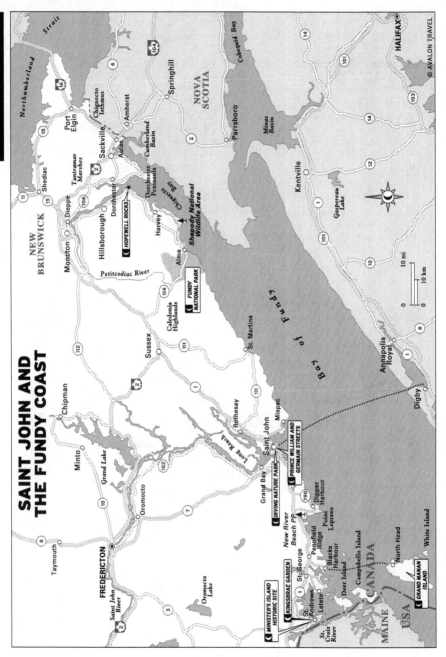

SAINT JOHN AND THE FUNDY COAST

© AVALON TRAVEL

St. Andrews—the province's definitive resort town on sheltered Passamaquoddy Bay—and the Fundy Isles, the archipelago (made up of Grand Manan, Deer, Campobello, and White Islands) that dangles into the sea alongside Maine's northernmost coast. The Upper Fundy area, situated at the coast's northeastern end, takes in Fundy National Park and several coastal bird sanctuaries.

PLANNING YOUR TIME

New Brunswick's 250-kilometer-long Fundy coastline is central to all of mainland Atlantic Canada, with the port city of Saint John roughly halfway between the U.S. border and the head of the bay. This is the place to explore historic **Prince William and Germain Streets,** get a taste of nature at **Irving Nature Park,** and take advantage of fine lodgings and restaurants. Everywhere else is within day-tripping distance of Saint John, but then you'd miss out on soaking up the old-fashioned resort atmosphere of **St. Andrews.** So plan on spending at least one night there, which will also allow time to visit **Kingsbrae Garden** and **Minister's Island Historic Site.** If you're driving up through Maine to Atlantic Canada, St. Andrews makes an ideal first stop. If you've rented a vehicle in Halifax, St. Andrews marks your turnaround point on a loop that incorporates a ferry trip from Digby to Saint John. Either way, on the north side of Saint John, plan on stops at **Fundy National Park** and **Hopewell Rocks** as you follow the Fundy Coast north to Moncton. By virtue of their location, the Fundy Isles require some extra time to reach, especially **Grand Manan Island,** but nature lovers will be rewarded with a magnificent display of birds, whales, and seals.

Saint John and Vicinity

Saint John (pop. 71,000), 110 kilometers south of Fredericton and 155 kilometers southwest of Moncton, ranks as New Brunswick's largest city, its major port, and its principal industrial center. It is also Canada's largest city in terms of area, sprawling across 321 square kilometers. The city perches on steep hills, laid out southwest to northeast across two peninsulas that almost mesh, like two hands about to meet in a handshake. The setting is among Atlantic Canada's most unusual—Saint John looks east across the spacious Saint John Harbour to the Bay of Fundy and is backed on the west by the confluence of the Saint John River and Kennebecasis Bay.

Saint John began as a collection of small Loyalist settlements. Today these settlements maintain their identities in the form of neighborhoods within greater Saint John. This accounts for numerous street-name duplications, a confusing fact of life when sightseeing across the oddly laid-out city. One Charlotte Street, for example, runs through the city's historic part, while another Charlotte Street is found in western Saint John. It helps to keep a map handy, or to just ask: the locals are sympathetic to the visitor's confusion.

Locals and visitors alike take full advantage of a revitalized waterfront precinct that includes the provincial museum, dining and shopping in Market Square, live outdoor entertainment, and the 2.3-kilometer Harbour Passage, a walking and biking trail that rims the waterfront.

HISTORY

On June 24, 1604, the feast day of St. John the Baptist, French explorer Samuel de Champlain sailed into the harbor area and named the river in the saint's honor. He dismissed the site, however, as unsuitable for settlement, and continued on to an island in the St. Croix River near St. Andrews.

Saint John's history as an Anglo settlement began with 14,000 Loyalists, who arrived by ship in 1783. The refugees quickly settled

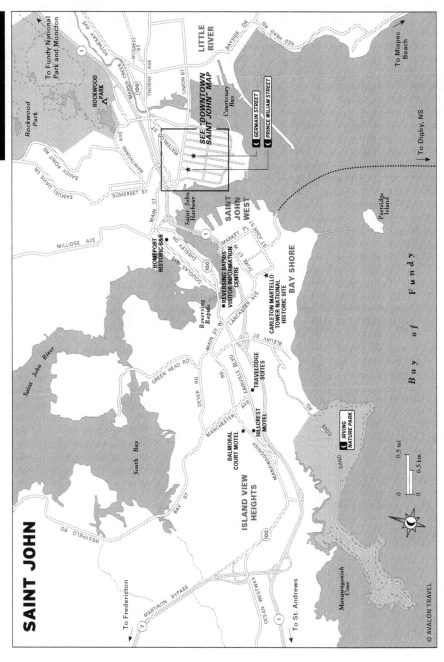

SAINT JOHN

To Fundy National Park and Moncton

ROCKWOOD PARK

Rockwood Park

LITTLE RIVER

To Mispec Beach

SEE 'DOWNTOWN SAINT JOHN' MAP

Courtenay Bay

GERMAIN STREET
PRINCE WILLIAM STREET

Saint John Harbour

SAINT JOHN WEST

Partridge Island

HOMEPORT HISTORIC B&B

Reversing Rapids

REVERSING RAPIDS VISITOR INFORMATION CENTRE

CARLETON MARTELLO TOWER NATIONAL HISTORIC SITE

BAY SHORE

Bay of Fundy

TRAVELODGE SUITES

HILLCREST MOTEL

BALMORAL COURT MOTEL

ISLAND VIEW HEIGHTS

IRVING NATURE PARK

To Fredericton

To St. Andrews

Manawagonish Cove

Saint John River

South Bay

0   0.5 mi
0   0.5 km

© AVALON TRAVEL

the fledgling town and spread out to found Carleton west of the harbor and Parrtown to the east. The city was incorporated in 1785, making it Canada's oldest. The port was an immediate economic success, and the Carleton Martello Tower was built to guard the harbor's shipping approaches during the War of 1812.

The city's next great wave of immigrants brought the Irish, who were fleeing poverty and persecution at home. Saint John's reputation as Canada's most Irish city began with a trickle of Irish in 1815; before the wave subsided in 1850, the city's 150,000 Irish outnumbered the Loyalists, and Saint John's religious complexion changed from Protestant to Roman Catholic.

Liverpool of America

Despite its early social woes, Saint John strode ahead economically and became known as the Liverpool of America. The *Marco Polo,* the world's fastest ship in its heyday, was launched in 1852, during an era when the port ranked third worldwide as a wooden ship builder. After steel-hulled steam vessels began to replace the great sailing ships in the 1860s, the city plunged into a decline, which was deepened by the Great Fire of 1877. The fire, in the Market Square area, raged for nine hours and left 18 people dead and another 13,000 homeless.

The blaze cost the city $28 million, but undaunted, Saint John replaced the damage with more elaborate, sturdier brick and stone buildings designed in the ornate Victorian style. The economic surge continued after New Brunswick joined the Confederation of Canada in 1867 and the nation's new railroads transported goods to Saint John for shipping.

World War II and Beyond

Saint John thrived during World War I as a shipping center for munitions, food, and troops bound for the Allied offensive in Europe. The port took an economic plunge during the Depression, further worsened by another devastating fire that destroyed port facilities. Prosperity returned during World War II;

© ANDREW HEMPSTEAD

The corner of King and Prince William Streets is a good place to begin your exploration of historic downtown Saint John.

the fortifications at Fort Dufferin, Partridge Island, Fort Mispec, and Carleton Martello Tower guarded the nation's shipping lifeline as German submarines roamed the Bay of Fundy.

Saint John modernized after the war. New Brunswick's native son billionaire, K. C. Irving, diversified his petroleum empire with the acquisition and expansion of the Saint John Shipbuilding facilities. The University of New Brunswick opened a campus at the city's north end; enrollment today is 1,150 full-time and 1,500 part-time students. Canada's Confederation centennial launched Saint John's rejuvenation in 1967. It continues to this day, most recently with the ambitious Harbour Passage waterfront promenade project.

GETTING ORIENTED

On a map, Saint John looks large and somewhat unmanageable, almost intimidating. Forget about Saint John's unusual shape and the soaring bridges that connect the city's parts.

Instead, concentrate on the main highways: The closely aligned Highway 1 and Highway 100, which parallel each other in most parts, are often the best routes for getting from one section of the city to another.

Tackle Saint John by areas. Most sightseeing is on the eastern peninsula in **uptown Saint John.** Access is easiest from Highway 1's Exits 121 or 125; the access roads peel down into the heart of downtown, centered on Market Square. The surrounding area is **Trinity Royal,** a national heritage preservation area protecting the original 20 blocks laid out by the Loyalists. You'll also know you've arrived by the street names: The early Loyalists called the area Parrtown, and the avenues were royally named as King, Princess, Queen, Prince William, and Charlotte Streets. This precinct is easily identified by distinctive blue and gold street signs.

Northern Saint John (the North End) lies on the highways' other side. **Rockwood Park,** one of Canada's largest municipal parks, dominates the area, with 870 wooded hectares speckled with lakes and an 18-hole golf course; numerous roads off Highway 1 feed into the park. This part of the city is also known to offer Saint John Harbour's best views; for a sublime overview, drive up to the **Fort Howe Lookout,** where timber blockhouses perch atop a rocky outcrop on Highway 1's northern side. Worthy hotels are nearby.

Western Saint John lies across the highway bridges on the western peninsula. Here you'll find some of the newer motels and a shopping mall along Highway 100, the area's commercial row, while Highway 1 heads west to St. Andrews. The residential area, which has several interesting bed-and-breakfasts, spreads out closer to the water, while the Bay Ferries ferry terminal (with service to Digby, Nova Scotia) is at the harbor's edge.

SIGHTS
Downtown

Hills aside, the following attractions are all within walking distance of one another. If the steep streets look daunting, flag a cab in front

© ANDREW HEMPSTEAD

The Harbour Passage walkway leads along the waterfront.

of the Hilton Saint John and ask the driver to drop you at King's Square ($5 with tip).

Downtown sightseeing starts at **Loyalist Plaza,** an outdoor strip filled with plants and seating that ends at the waterfront. It's a good place to get oriented by visiting the information center (in Market Square) and taking the **Harbour Passage** waterfront promenade around the head of the harbor. This paved walking/biking trail leads 2.3 kilometers to a pavilion from which views extend back across to downtown.

NEW BRUNSWICK MUSEUM

The province's prime resource for fine arts and natural history lore is this museum inside Market Square (St. Patrick St., 506/643-2300; Mon.–Fri. 9 A.M.–5 P.M., Sat. 10 A.M.–5 P.M., Sun. noon–5 P.M.; adult $8, senior $6, child $4.50). One of Canada's oldest museums, its displays are spread through three floors packed with elegant ship models, shipbuilding tools, war memorabilia, stuffed birds and beasts, agricultural and domestic implements, you name it. There's a hands-on Discovery Centre for kids and a bookstore that stocks literature about the province.

BARBOUR'S GENERAL STORE

Across Loyalist Plaza from Market Square, the essence of old-time New Brunswick is re-created at this restored country store and museum (506/658-2939; mid-May–mid-Oct. daily 9 A.M.–6 P.M.; free), which was moved from upriver at Sheffield. Inside are 2,000 artifacts typical of the period from 1840 to 1940, as well as a restored turn-of-the-twentieth-century barbershop in the back room. Next door, peek into the bright red schoolhouse, which was also moved to the site from rural New Brunswick.

◀ PRINCE WILLIAM AND GERMAIN STREETS

A block up from Market Square, these two parallel streets delineate the commercial heart

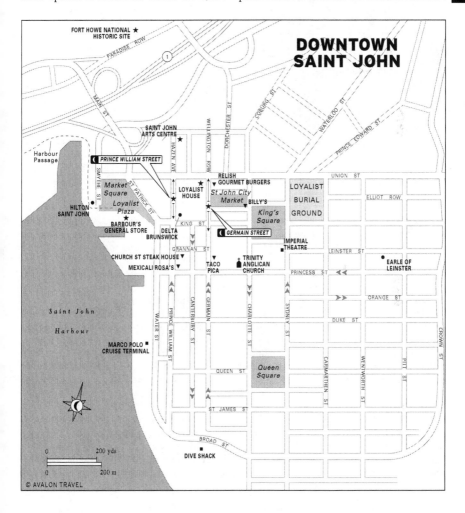

DOWNTOWN SAINT JOHN

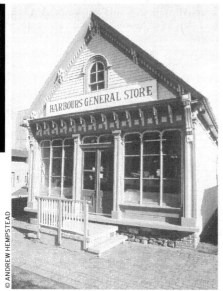

© ANDREW HEMPSTEAD

Barbour's General Store

of old Saint John. Following the devastating fire of June 1877, the city hurried to rebuild itself in even grander style. The stone and brick edifices along Prince William Street are a splendid farrago of architectural styles, incorporating Italianate facades, Corinthian columns, Queen Anne Revival elements, scowling gargoyles, and other decorative details. One of the country's finest surviving examples of 19th-century streetscape, this was the first "national historic street" in Canada. Some good art galleries and craft shops are ensconced here among the other businesses. Two blocks east, Germain Street is the more residential counterpoint, proffering a number of opulent townhouses.

LOYALIST HOUSE NATIONAL HISTORIC SITE

This simple, white clapboard Georgian-style house (120 Union St., 506/652-3590; mid-May–June Mon.–Fri. 10 A.M.–5 P.M., July–mid-Sept. daily 10 A.M.–5 P.M.; adult $5, child

$2) was built between 1810 and 1817 by pioneer David Merrit, and it remained in his family for five generations. Having survived the 1877 fire and now meticulously restored, it's the oldest unaltered building in the city. The original front door with brass knocker opens into an authentic evocation of the early Loyalist years, furnished with Sheraton, Empire, and Duncan Phyfe antiques.

SAINT JOHN ARTS CENTRE

One block west of the Jewish museum, the grandiose former Carnegie Library (20 Hazen Ave., 506/633-4870; June–early Sept. daily 10 A.M.–5 P.M., early Sept.–May Tues.–Sun. 11:30 A.M.–4:30 P.M.; free) is now a cultural complex. Inside, six galleries (including the City of Saint John Gallery) hold frequently changing fine arts and photography exhibits.

SAINT JOHN CITY MARKET

For a visual and culinary treat, spend some time at Saint John's Old City Market (47 Charlotte St., 506/658-2820; Mon.–Thurs. 7:30 A.M.–6 P.M., Fri. to 7 P.M., Sat. to 5 P.M.; free), spanning a whole city block between Charlotte and Germain Streets. The setting is impressive. The original ornate iron gates stand at each entrance, and there's usually a busker or two working the crowd. Inside the airy stone building, local shipbuilders framed the expansive ceiling in the form of an inverted ship's hull. "Market Street," the market's central, widest aisle, divides the space in half; alongside the adjacent aisles, the bustling stalls stand cheek-by-jowl, their tables groaning with wares. Notice the building's pitched floor, a convenient arrangement on the slanted hillside that makes hosing the floor easier after the market closes each day.

The market is a great venue for people-watching and for sampling fresh baked goods, cheeses, seafood, meat, and produce. If you haven't yet tried dulse, a leather-tough purple seaweed that's harvested from the Bay of Fundy, dried, and sold in little packages for a dollar or two, here's your chance. Splendid, reasonably priced crafts have a sizable niche here, too.

KING'S SQUARE AND THE
LOYALIST BURIAL GROUND
Across Charlotte Street from the City Market are two maple-shaded, vest-pocket green spaces situated on separate kitty-corner blocks. At King's Square, the walkways are laid out like the stripes on the British Union Jack, radiating from the 1908 bandstand, the site of summertime concerts.

Across Sydney Street is the Loyalist Burial Ground, a surprisingly cheerful place with benches and flower gardens, scattered with old-style headstones dating back to 1784.

As busy as the square and burial ground are—alive with schoolchildren on field trips, bantering seniors, and moms with strollers—**Queen's Square,** three blocks south, is virtually deserted.

TRINITY ANGLICAN CHURCH
A victim of the city's historic fires, this handsome Loyalist church (115 Charlotte St., 506/693-8558; Mon.–Fri. 9 A.M.–3 P.M.; free) was built in 1791, rebuilt in 1856, and rebuilt again in 1880 after the Great Fire. The sanctuary's famed treasure is the House of Hanover Royal Coat of Arms from the reign of George I, which was rescued by fleeing Loyalists from the Boston Council Chamber in 1783 and rescued again from the 1877 runaway fire.

West of Downtown
FORT HOWE NATIONAL
HISTORIC SITE LOOKOUT
The blockhouse of 1777 did double duty as harbor defense and city jail. The structure itself is a replica, but the rocky promontory site on Magazine Street nonetheless offers an excellent panoramic view of the city and harbor. To get there from downtown, cross the highway along Main Street.

REVERSING RAPIDS
If ever there were a contest for Most Overhyped

Tourist Attraction, this site would win the grand prize. Tour buses and out-of-province license plates pack the parking lot, disgorging gaggles of camera-toting visitors to see …what? At low tide, the Bay of Fundy lies 4.4 meters below the Saint John River, and the river flows out to sea across a small falls (more like a rapids) here. During the slack tide, the sea and the river levels are equal and the rapids disappear. Then, as the slack tide grows to high tide, the waters of the rising sea enter Saint John Harbour, muscling the river inland for 100 kilometers and creating some turbulent rapids. It's an unspectacular sight, and even the minimal physical science interest can't be appreciated unless you're willing to hang around for 12 hours and watch the tide go through a full cycle. Nevertheless, throngs of visitors line up here for the requisite photo opportunity.

What all the hype does accomplish, however, is to draw all those tourists in to the friendly and helpful **Reversing Rapids Visitor Information Centre** (Fallsview Dr., 506/658-2937; mid-May–mid-Oct. daily 8 A.M.–8 P.M.), which is probably as good a place as any to get information about the area. If you're interested in a capsule version of the sea and river encounter, check out the audiovisual ($2.50). To get there from downtown, cross Highway 1 via Main Street and turn left on Clesley Drive. The complex is on the far side of the bridge spanning the river.

For a reverse angle on Reversing Rapids, go to **Fallsview Park,** which overlooks the spectacle from the east side of the river, off Douglas Avenue.

CARLETON MARTELLO TOWER
NATIONAL HISTORIC SITE
The massive circular stone tower (Fundy Dr. at Whipple St., Saint John West, 506/636-4011; June–early Oct. daily 10 A.M.–5:30 P.M.; adult $4, senior $3.50, child $2) served as a harbor defense outpost from 1812 and was declared a national historic site in 1924. The superstructure above it was a military intelligence center during World War II. Within, stone staircases

connect the restored quarters and powder magazine. The observation decks provide splendid views of the harbor.

PARTRIDGE ISLAND

This island near the mouth of Saint John Harbour, a national and provincial historic site and now a coast guard light station, was a quarantine station for almost a million arriving immigrants during the 19th and 20th centuries, many of whom arrived sick with cholera, typhus, and smallpox. Some 2,000 newcomers who never made it any farther are buried here in six graveyards. A Celtic cross was erected for the Irish refugees, and a memorial stone commemorates Jewish immigrants. From the early 1800s up to 1947, the island was used as a military fortification. Most of the old wooden buildings have now been destroyed, and the island is off-limits to the public. If you're catching the ferry to Digby (Nova Scotia), stand on the starboard (right) side as the vessel pulls away from the terminal and you'll get a great view of the island.

RECREATION

A visit to Saint John is about soaking up history and enjoying the services affiliated with a city, but there are a few things to keep you busy beyond sightseeing. The two parks detailed below have good walking trails, **Rockwood Park Golf Course** (506/634-0090; greens fee $39) offers a challenging tree-lined layout, and there are water sports to try.

Parks
ROCKWOOD PARK

This huge woodland park (506/658-2883; daily dawn–dusk), speckled with 13 lakes and laced with foot and horse trails, is across Highway 1 from downtown, with access from Exits 123, 125, and 128. In spring, yellow lady's slipper and colorful wild orchid varieties bloom on the forest floor, and the gardens and arboretum are in their full glory. Activities in summer include fishing, boating, swimming, bird-watching, hiking, horseback riding, golfing at the 18-hole course, picnicking at lakeside

tables, and camping. In winter, the ice skaters come out and the trails are taken over by cross-country skiers.

Cherry Brook Zoo (901 Foster Thurston Rd., 506/634-1440; daily 10 A.M.–dusk; adult $10.50, senior $8.50, child $5.50), at the park's northern end, off Sandy Point Road, is stocked with lions, leopards, zebras, and other exotic animals. The zoo includes Vanished Kingdom Park, where you find replicas of extinct animals.

⟨⟨ IRVING NATURE PARK

Irving Nature Park occupies an unlikely setting. The remote reserve encompasses an entire peninsula dangling into Saint John Harbour, the province's busiest port. At the harbor's northeastern corner rises the skyline of New Brunswick's largest city. Across the harbor's center, oceangoing vessels enter and leave the port. Yet at the harbor's western corner, this speck of natural terrain remains blissfully remote and as undeveloped as it was when the city's founding Loyalists arrived centuries ago.

© ANDREW HEMPSTEAD

Irving Nature Park

To get there, take Highway 1 out of the city to western Saint John and watch for the Catherwood Street turnoff (Exit 119). The narrow road angles south off the highway, takes a jog to the right (west), descends through a residential area, and then lopes across an undeveloped marshland to the 225-hectare reserve. A sandy beach backed by the Saints Rest Marsh heralds the park's entrance. Many visitors park at the bottom of the hill and continue on foot. It is also possible to continue by road into the park, to a parking lot 500 meters from the beach, or to follow a one-way road that encircles the entire headland. Trails probe the park's interior and also wander off to parallel the water.

The reserve's mixed ecosystem offers interesting trekking terrain and draws songbirds, waterfowl, and migratory seabirds. More than 240 bird species are seen regularly; 365 species have been sighted over the past 20 years. Rare red crossbills and peregrine falcons are occasionally spotted in the marsh. Eastern North America's largest cormorant colony lies offshore on Manawagonish Island. Semipalmated plovers like the reserve's quiet beaches and tidal flats. You can count on sandpiper varieties on the beach in July, greater shearwaters and Wilson's stormy petrels gliding across the water during summer, and a spectacular show of loons, grebes, and scoters during the autumn migration along the Atlantic flyway. Birds are the most noticeable but by no means the only wildlife to be found here. Deer, porcupines, red squirrels, and snowshoe hares inhabit the reserve. And starfish and sea urchins laze in the tidal pools.

Water Sports
The **Dive Shack** (9 Lower Cove Loop, 506/634-8265; Mon.–Fri. 10 A.M.–6 P.M., Sat. 10 A.M.–3 P.M.) is the city's prime source for dive trips to the Bay of Fundy. The shop also rents equipment, runs courses, and offers weekend charters. Lower Cove Loop is an extension of Water Street south through downtown.

The top-notch facilities at the **Canada Games Aquatic Centre** (50 Union St., 506/658-4715)

include a 50-meter pool with five diving boards, two shallower pools, two water slides, whirlpools, saunas, a fitness room, and a cafeteria. A day-use pass to the pool and fitness center costs $12; for the pool alone, it's $7.50.

You'll find supervised swimming at Fisher Lake in **Rockwood Park,** at **Dominion Park** in Saint John West, and at **Little River Reservoir** off Loch Lomond Road in the city's eastern area. **Mispec Beach** at Saint John Harbour's eastern edge is unsupervised, and the water is cold, but it's a nice spot on a warm day and provides close-up views of ships from around the world entering and leaving the harbor. To get there, take Union Street and make a sharp right turn to Bayside Drive, and then turn onto Red Head Road.

ENTERTAINMENT AND EVENTS
Performing Arts
The city's pride and joy is the immaculately restored 1913 **Imperial Theatre** (24 King Square S., 506/674-4100). In its heyday, the theater hosted performances by the likes of Ethel Barrymore, John Philip Sousa, and Harry Houdini. After closing in the 1950s, it was reopened and used by the Full Gospel Assembly Pentecostal Church for 25 years. In 1994, decade-long renovations to restore the theater to its former glory were completed. Today it's once again the star venue of Saint John's performing arts scene, hosting concerts by Symphony New Brunswick, stage productions of Theatre New Brunswick, and a variety of touring performers.

Pubs and Nightclubs
Saint John may seem all historic and charming during the day, but remember that it's primarily an international port. Be careful after dark, especially at the south end of downtown. That said, bars and restaurants along Market Square have a beautiful outlook with lots of outdoor tables that stay full with locals and visitors well into the night on summer weekends, when musicians take to an outdoor stage. **Grannan's** (St. Patrick St., 506/634-1555; daily from

© ANDREW HEMPSTEAD

Built in 1913, the Imperial Theatre is now fully restored.

Festivals and Events

In addition to free evening entertainment in Loyalist Plaza, summer brings the **Salty Jam** (www.saltyjam.com) music festival to Market Square, Pugsley Wharf, and other venues the second weekend of July.

The five-day **Atlantic National Exhibition** finishes the summer with a super-size county fair geared to families. It runs from late August to early September at the Exhibition Grounds (McAllister Dr., 506/633-2020, www.eprraceway.com).

On the fourth Sunday in October, the Marco Polo Cruise Terminal (111 Water St.) fills with the smells of the best in local cooking for the **Fundy Food Festival** (www.fundyfoodfestival.com). Admission is $5, and for nominal extra charges you can sample creations from local restaurants and food suppliers.

SHOPPING

The city's main shopping district—along Charlotte, Union, Princess, Germain, and Prince William Streets—is filled with interesting outlets selling everything from Inuit art to Irish tartan. The local penchant for high-quality weaving and handmade apparel is particularly evident at **Handworks Gallery** (12 King St., 506/652-9787; Mon.–Sat. 10 A.M.–6 A.M.). In the vicinity is one of Atlantic Canada's preeminent antique dealers, **Tim Isaac Antiques** (213 Wentworth St., 506/652-3222; Mon.–Sat. 10 A.M.–4 P.M.). Saint John is Canada's most Irish city, and Celtic wares are abundant. **House of Tara** (72 Prince William St., 506/634-8272; closed Sunday) is stuffed with Irish imports, including plentiful jewelry and clothing (the tweeds are particularly attractive) and Belleek pottery.

ACCOMMODATIONS AND CAMPING

Ideally, you'll want to be within walking distance of historic old Saint John and the harbor. The area's bed-and-breakfasts often provide sumptuous accommodations for lower cost

11:30 A.M.) forms a hub for the many nearby bars of many moods, and its indoor lounge has an inviting pub ambience. Adjacent **Cougar's Lounge** (506/693-6666; daily 11 A.M.–2 A.M.) and **Saint John Ale House** (506/657-2337; daily 11 A.M.–2 A.M.) also have wide portions of Loyalist Plaza packed with outdoor furniture, with the former offering live music many nights. Toward the water, **Brigantine Lounge** (Hilton Saint John, Market Sq., 506/632-8564; daily 11:30 A.M.–midnight) is less pretentious than you might expect and has a menu encompassing everything from nachos to a bourbon-glazed striploin.

The Historic Trinity Royal area, bounded by Prince William, Princess, King, and Germain Streets, is another nightlife center, with nightclubs, pubs, lounges, and sports bars. One of the more welcoming places is **O'Leary's** (46 Princess St., 506/634-7135), a convivial Irish pub with the obligatory Guinness on tap and the sound of Celtic musicians filling the room Thursday–Saturday.

than many hotels. Lodgings beyond walking distance include the Fort Howe–area hotels, with great harbor vistas at reasonable prices, and the many budget choices on Manawagonish Avenue in Saint John West.

$50-100

Of the bed-and-breakfast lodgings clustered near King's Square, none are better value than **Earle of Leinster** (96 Leinster St., 506/652-3275, www.earleofleinster.com; $85 s, $95–100 d), with congenial hosts and a very central location. This gracious brick Victorian townhouse has seven rooms with private baths. One of the rooms is a family suite. Amenities include laundry facilities, a game room with a pool table, a courtyard, and business services. Rates include a full breakfast.

Around five kilometers from downtown, Manawagonish Avenue is lined with inexpensive motels—a reminder of the time that this was the main route west out of the city. To get there from the west, take Exit 100 from Highway 1 and follow Ocean Westaway toward the city; from downtown, take Exit 119 and follow Catherwood Street north. Choices in the $80–100 s or d range include **Balmoral Court Motel** (1284 Manawagonish Ave., 506/672-3019) and **Hillcrest Motel** (1315 Manawagonish Ave., 506/672-5310).

$100-150

Canada Select gives its ultimate five-star rating only sparingly, but **◖ Homeport Historic Bed & Breakfast** (80 Douglas Ave., 506/672-7255 or 888/678-7678, www.homeport.nb.ca; $109–175 s or d) deserves every one of its five. Set high on the hill overlooking the harbor and city, this lodging combines two mansions dating from the mid-1800s. From the impressive collection of antiques to the super-comfortable beds to the decanter of port left in the lobby for guests returning from dinner, it is obvious hosts Ralph and Karen Holyoke know how to make their guests feel like they're paying a lot more than they really are. Standard rooms are $109 s or d, but the Luxury Rooms at $149 are

well worth the extra money. Rates include a full breakfast.

Travelodge and Suites (1011 Fairville Blvd., 506/635-0400 or 800/525-4055, www.travelodge.com; from $120 s or d) is your typical midrange roadside motel, with clean, comfortable, and practical guest rooms. Standard rooms are $120 s or d, but the much-larger suites, with separate bedrooms and king beds, are a good value at $145. A complimentary light breakfast is laid out for guests. Take Exit 117 from Highway 1.

$150-200

Occupying a prime waterfront locale and linked to Market Square by an elevated walkway is **◖ Hilton Saint John** (1 Market Sq., 506/693-8484 or 800/561-8282, www.hilton.com; $195 s or d), a 12-story high-rise dating to the mid-1980s. Most of its 200 rooms have water views and windows that open. They come with all the usual niceties—daily newspaper, coffeemaker, hair dryer, and more—while a waterfront restaurant, a lounge, a fitness room, and an indoor pool are downstairs. Check online for packages that include a buffet breakfast.

Rack rates at the **Delta Brunswick** (39 King St., 506/648-1981 or 888/890-3222, www.deltahotels.com) may be almost $200 per night, but reserve online and you'll pay less. Part of the Brunswick Square Mall and one block back from the harbor, this modern hotel has 254 elegant rooms, as well as an indoor pool, a fitness room, and a restaurant and lounge.

Campground

A five-minute drive from downtown, **Rockwood Park Campground** (124 Lake Drive S., 506/652-4050; May–Sept.; $23–33) has more than 200 sites, most with electricity and water. Amenities include big communal bathrooms, kitchen shelters, fireplaces, and a campers' canteen. Available recreation includes golfing at the nearby course, swimming, boating at the lake, and hiking on trails around the lake. The easiest way to get to the campground is to take Highway 1 Exit 121 or 125 and follow the signs north. No reservations are taken, but the sites rarely fill.

FOOD

Market Square is the most obvious and convenient choice for visitors looking for a meal, but head uphill into the heart of downtown and you'll come across restaurants that trade on good food and prices alone.

Market

You won't know which way to turn once you've walked through the doors of the **❰** **Saint John City Market** (47 Charlotte St., 506/658-2820; Mon.–Thurs. 7:30 A.M.–6 P.M., Fri. to 7 P.M., Sat. to 5 P.M.), a city institution. Choose from a couple of old-fashioned cafés; a seafood market with live lobsters (they'll box them for you) and mussels for just $2 per pound; a delicatessen with sliced meats and gourmet cheeses; and Wild Carrot Café, boasting healthy juices and muffins.

© ANDREW HEMPSTEAD

For the best variety of dining options, head to the waterfront and Market Square.

Seafood

Grannan's (1 Market Sq., 506/634-1555; Mon.–Wed. 11 A.M.–11 P.M., Thurs.–Sat. 11 A.M.–midnight, Sun. noon–10 P.M.; $18–38) is one of the Market Square restaurants with as many tables outside as in. The specialty is seafood, and everything is good. The chowder is expensive but delicious, while mains include blackened Creole salmon, seafood casserole, and snow crab.

❰ **Billy's** (49 Charlotte St., 506/672-3474; Mon.–Thurs. 11 A.M.–10 P.M., Fri.–Sat. 11 A.M.–10 P.M., Sun. 4–9 P.M.; $18–33) is tucked away at the back of the Saint John City Market. It's part fish market, part restaurant, so you know everything will be fresh. Everything is good—Atlantic Canada delicacies include Malpeque oysters served raw in their shells, fish cakes, seafood chowder, lobster-stuffed haddock, Digby scallops sautéed in a pesto sauce, blackened salmon with an apple-cinnamon glaze, and a creamy shrimp risotto.

Burgers

For the city's best burgers, head to **Relish Gourmet Burgers** (26 Germain St., 506/645-2333; Mon.–Sat. 11:30 A.M.–8 P.M., Sun. 11:30 A.M.–6 P.M.; $9–13.50), a modern space where options are as simple as the Simpleton and as creative as the Harvest Jazz (a turkey burger with blue cheese, havarti, caramelized onion, and walnut pesto). Delicious milkshakes and enthusiastic service are bonuses.

Thai

Saint John proves it's up on restaurant trends at **❰** **Lemongrass** (1 Market Sq., 506/657-8424; daily lunch and dinner; $17–23), a warmly decorated dining room in the bustling Market Square complex. You can't miss with *tod mun pla* (fish cakes infused with red curry and coriander) and either *phad yum* (seafood curry with lime leaves) or *hor neing pla* (steamed haddock with lemongrass and other herbs wrapped in a banana leaf) as a main.

Mexican and Central American

Just a block off King Street, the city hustle and

bustle drops off dramatically. Small, bright, and casual 🔲 **Taco Pica** (96 Germain St., 506/633-8492; Mon.–Sat. 10 A.M.–10 P.M., mains $12–19) is a real find on a quiet side street in the Trinity Royal historic area, away from the tourist traffic. The Guatemalan proprietor offers a mouthwatering menu of recipes from his homeland, as well as dishes from Mexico and Spain. Try the *pepian* (a spicy Guatemalan beef stew) or Spanish paella, washed down with a Mexican beer.

Mexicali Rosa's (88 Prince William St., 506/652-5252; Mon.–Sat. 11:30 A.M.–11 P.M., Sun. noon–10 P.M.; $9–19) is a popular hangout for locals looking for a Mexican meal in casual surroundings. For those on a budget, the chili con carne in a sourdough bread bowl ($9) is tempting, or splash out on creative offerings like Drunken Shrimp Fajitas ($19).

Hotel Dining

The dining rooms in the major hotels are also safe bets, though pricier. **Shucker's** (Delta Brunswick, 39 King St., 506/648-1981; daily 7–11 A.M. and 5–9 P.M.; $17–30) offers tempting selections such as grilled Fundy Bay salmon fillet splashed with lemon butter or served with capers and cream. An alternative "Heart Smart" menu features low-fat poultry, seafood, and fruit salads. Tuesday–Thursday lunch is a buffet.

The maritime-themed **Turn of the Tide** (Saint John Hilton, Market Sq., 506/632-8564; daily 6:30–11:30 A.M.; breakfast buffet $17) is right on the waterfront, with awesome views and a expansive breakfast buffet to match. Also in the hotel is the **Brigantine Lounge** (Hilton Saint John, Market Sq., 506/632-8564; daily 11:30 A.M.–midnight; $14–29), which opens to a dockside patio. Menu highlights include thin-crust pizzas, mussels steamed in wheat beer, and mushroom-crusted rack of lamb.

INFORMATION AND SERVICES

Tourist Information

Tourism Saint John (506/658-2855 or 866/463-8639, www.tourismsaintjohn.com)

does a great job of promoting the city, and its helpful website should be your first point of contact in planning your trip. It operates the city's main **Visitor Information Centre** (daily 9 A.M.–6 P.M., summer daily until 8 P.M.) at the eastern entrance to Market Square; it faces the corner of St. Patrick and King Streets.

Books and Bookstores

Saint John Library (1 Market Sq., 506/643-7220; Mon.–Wed. 9 A.M.–5 P.M., Thurs.–Fri. 9 A.M.–9 P.M., Sat. 9 A.M.–5 P.M.) is in the downtown Market Square complex. It holds a good selection of New Brunswick titles and offers free Internet access for visitors.

To purchase books about the province's natural, human, and cultural history, head for the **New Brunswick Museum,** right by the library in Market Square (506/643-2300). **Coles** has three mall locations within the city, including downtown at Brunswick Square (39 King St., 506/658-9114).

Post Office

The main **post office** is at 125 Rothesay Avenue. **Lawton's Drugs** (Brunswick Sq., 506/634-1422) serves as one of the city's numerous retail postal outlets and has longer hours. **Shoppers Drug Stores** also have postal service outlets.

Internet Services

Downtown hotels and most bed-and-breakfasts have wireless or modem Internet access, or head to **Saint John Library** (1 Market Sq., 506/643-7220; Mon.–Wed. 9 A.M.–5 P.M., Thurs.–Fri. 9 A.M.–9 P.M., Sat. 9 A.M.–5 P.M.), where getting online is free.

Emergency Services

Saint John Regional Hospital (400 University Ave., 506/648-6000) is on the university campus near Rockwood Park. For the police or other emergencies, call 911. Convenient pharmacies include **Lawton's Drugs** (Brunswick Sq., 39 King St., 506/634-1422) and **Guardian Drugs** (114 River Valley Dr., 506/738-8406).

GETTING THERE

Air

Saint John Airport is 16 kilometers east of downtown. The airport is served by **Air Canada** (888/247-2262) from Halifax, Toronto, and Montréal. Car rental companies represented are Avis, Budget, Hertz, and National, while other airport services include a restaurant and gift shop.

Taxis wait outside the airport for flight arrivals; the 25-minute cab ride to Market Square costs about $35.

Bus

Saint John Bus Terminal (199 Chesley Dr., 506/648-3500) is the arrival and departure point for **Acadian** buses to and from Bangor (Maine), Fredericton, and Moncton. If you've arrived in Saint John by bus and catch the ferry to Digby (Nova Scotia), there will be an Acadian bus waiting to transport you to Halifax.

Ferry

Bay Ferries (902/245-2116 or 888/249-7245, www.nfl-bay.com) sails the *Princess of Acadia* between Saint John and Digby (Nova Scotia) year-round, up to three times daily in summer. It's a good option if you've driven through New Brunswick and want to explore Nova Scotia's Fundy Coast. The crossing is 3.5 hours (adult $41, senior and youth $31, child under five $5, vehicle $82 plus a $20 fuel surcharge). To get to the terminal from Highway 1, take Exit 120 and follow the signs south along Market Street. The terminal has no café, so if you're looking for a snack while waiting in line, stop at the Tim Hortons along Market Street.

GETTING AROUND

Saint John is a walking town in the historic area, but beyond there you'll need wheels. Highway 1 serves as the city's high-speed expressway and routes east–west traffic through Saint John from St. Stephen and Moncton. Highway 100 is the city's local traffic route, and it serves as a feeder route for Highway 7 to and from Fredericton. Driving is slow going

most everywhere in Saint John, but it's worst during the 7–9 A.M. and 4:30–6 P.M. rush hours.

Parking garages and lots in the historic area are plentiful and inexpensive. Outdoor lots cost $1 an hour; indoor lots are slightly higher. Coming off Highway 1 at Exit 122, take the first right, and you'll pass outdoor pay parking on your right, or continue to the bottom of the hill and turn left for underground parking.

Bus

Saint John Transit (506/658-4700; $2.75 per sector) buses run throughout the city (Mon.–Fri. 6 A.M.–midnight, with limited service on weekends). The company also offers two-hour guided bus tours of Saint John twice daily (at 10 A.M. and 1 P.M.) from late June to September. The cost is adult $20, child $5.

Taxi

Cabs wait in front of the Delta and Hilton hotels, or call **Saint John Taxi** (506/693-0000), **Diamond Taxi** (506/648-8888), or **Royal Taxi** (506/652-5050). Fares are based on 14 city zones; expect to pay around $8 from Market Square to Fort Howe and $35 to the airport.

SAINT JOHN TO ST. ANDREWS

In addition to the intrinsic beauty of the coast—with thick forests growing right down to the rocky shoreline—several detours spice up the 90-kilometer drive west to St. Andrews.

Point Lepreau and Vicinity

The first spot of note west of Saint John is **Point Lepreau Nuclear Generating Station,** at the end of Highway 790. It opened in 1980 as Canada's first nuclear power station. It currently supplies 30 percent of New Brunswick's power needs.

A few kilometers beyond Highway 790, **New River Beach Provincial Park** (506/755-4042; May–Oct.) lies alongside the highway and has picnic tables, a long curving sandy beach, hiking trails through bogs and spruce woodlands, and boat launching facilities.

A good-value accommodation along this stretch of highway is the **Clipper Shipp Beach Motel** (506/755-2211; Mar.–Nov.; $80 s or d). The rooms are very basic—you're paying for a stunning waterfront location.

St. George

The most impressive sight at St. George, 32 kilometers before reaching St. Andrews, is the thundering granite gorge of **Magaguadavic Falls.** Visitors can park and walk down a staircase beside the falls to watch salmon swimming upstream past a viewing window. The specialty at **Oven Head Salmon Smokers** (101 Ovenhead Rd., 506/755-2507; Mon.–Sat. 8 A.M.–5 P.M.) is Atlantic salmon, cold-smoked to perfection over hickory and oak chips. The smokehouse wholesales to culinary notables such as the Fairmont Algonquin.

St. George is also the place to turn off Highway 1 for the short drive to the Deer Island ferry terminus at Letete. Highways 772 and 776 lead to Black Bay, picturesque **Blacks Harbour** (terminus for the Grand Manan Island ferry), and a welter of other islets.

St. Andrews and Vicinity

St. Andrews by the Sea, as it is marketed by the local tourism authority, is an immensely attractive seaside town (pop. 1,800), 90 kilometers west of Saint John. New Brunswick's first—and now definitive—resort town, St. Andrews sits at the end of a peninsula dangling into tranquil Passamaquoddy Bay, sheltered from the tumultuous Fundy by Deer Island and Letang Peninsula. The resort crowd revels in St. Andrews's version of old-time velvet-glove Canadiana, especially visible at the many upscale lodgings.

© ANDREW HEMPSTEAD

Water Street, St. Andrews

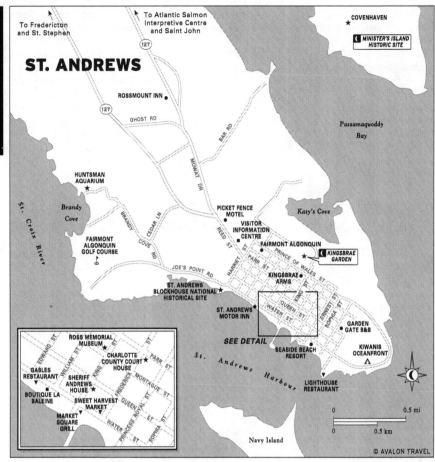

History

The town has a special, almost sacred historic status among New Brunswickers. It was founded by Loyalists who sailed into the Fundy and followed the coastal curve to the peninsula's tip in 1783. The courageous journey was a technical wonder. The settlers, originally from England's former colonies farther south, had moved to what they believed was Canada at Castine, Maine. But a subsequent international boundary decision forced them to relocate once again. The pro-Crown settlers reloaded convoys with all their possessions, disassembled houses and reloaded the structures on barges, and set sail for a safe homeland. St. Andrews was their creation. Most every street is named for George III or one of his kin. A few Loyalist houses remain and sit cheek-by-jowl with similar New England–style houses fronting narrow residential streets.

SIGHTS

For a town that encourages relaxation, there's a lot to see and do. Many historic attractions are within walking distance of downtown accommodations, while others are just a short drive away. You could easily spend two days in town and still not have time to golf the hallowed fairways of Fairmont Algonquin Golf Course or go whale-watching. One of the most interesting things to do in St. Andrews is to watch the effect of the tide. I'm not suggesting you sit at the end of the Town Wharf for six hours, but take a peek at low or high tide, and then return six hours later—the effect is amazing.

Historic Downtown

St. Andrews is a historic gem. Nearly half the buildings in the town core date back more than 100 years, and most have been maintained or restored to mint condition. Water Street is the main avenue, following the shoreline through the five-block commercial district.

In the town's center, **Sheriff Andrews House** (63 King St., 506/529-5080; late June–early Sept. Mon.–Sat. 9:30 A.M.–4:30 P.M., Sun. 1–4:30 P.M.; donation) offers an attractive visual insight into the early Loyalist era. Costumed guides will show you around the county sheriff's neoclassical-style 1820 house, which is simply but elegantly furnished in local period style.

The whitewashed **Charlotte County Court House** (Frederick St., 506/529-3843; July–Aug. Mon.–Sat. 9:30 A.M.–noon and 1–4:30 P.M.; free) dates to 1840 and is thought to be the country's oldest courthouse in continuous use.

Ross Memorial Museum (188 Montague St., 506/529-5124; early June–early Oct. Mon.–Sat. 10 A.M.–4:30 P.M.; donation), in an early-19th-century neoclassical brick home, preserves the furniture, porcelains, rugs, mirrors, paintings, and other items of Henry and Sarah Ross, discerning collectors of antiques and objets d'art.

🅲 Kingsbrae Garden

Kingsbrae Garden (220 King St., 506/529-3335; mid-May–mid-Oct. daily 9 A.M.–6 P.M.; adult $14, senior and child $10) incorporates

gardens that were once part of the Kingsbrae Arms estate, as well as additional land, to create 11 hectares of tranquility on the hill above downtown. It is home to more than 2,000 species—a place to feast your eyes on rhododendrons, roses, an orchard, a working windmill, an Acadian coastal forest, and a children's garden featuring miniature houses. The complex also includes a shop selling floral-themed gifts and a café overlooking the garden.

St. Andrews Blockhouse National Historic Site

A pleasant walk along Water Street from downtown will lead you to St. Andrews Blockhouse (454 Whipple St., 506/529-4270; June–Aug. daily 10 A.M.–6 P.M.; adult $1, child $0.40). The fortification, the last survivor of 12 similar structures, was intended to protect the town from attack in the War of 1812, but nary a shot was fired in battle at this site. The interior depicts the War of 1812 era with re-created soldiers' quarters.

Even if you're not hot on history, the site is worth exploring for the wide grassy expanse out

St. Andrews Blockhouse National Historic Site

ST. CROIX ISLAND

In 1604, a French exploration party of 79 led by Samuel de Champlain sailed into the Bay of Fundy and named the Saint John River. After rejecting the site of the present city of Saint John as a proper spot for a settlement, the group spent the bitterly cold winter of 1604-1605 on Douchet's Island in the St. Croix River. The settlement marked the beginning of a French presence in North America. After a bitter winter in which hunger and scurvy claimed 35 lives, the remaining settlers packed up and headed for Nova Scotia's more agreeable side of the Fundy. There they established Port-Royal, the early hub of "Acadia," the name they gave this part of eastern Canada.

The St. Croix River, which drains into the Bay of Fundy at St. Andrews, forms the international border, and the site of the settlement is now protected as **St. Croix Island International Historic Site.** Beside Highway 127, nine kilometers north of St. Andrews, where views extend over the island, interpretive boards tell the story of the settlement. On the U.S. side, there's a viewing platform 13 kilometers south of Calais.

front, which edges the St. Croix River. Time your visit for the ebb (receding) tide, and you'll watch the revealing of a rocky peninsula and pools that are fully submerged at high tide.

◖ Minister's Island Historic Site

This 200-hectare island (506/529-5081; adult $15, senior and student $10) in Passamaquoddy Bay was where Canadian Pacific Railway magnate William Van Horne built his summer retreat, **Covenhoven.** Completed in 1903, the 50-room home was built of locally quarried sandstone, and it, a windmill, a tidal swimming pool, and a barn remain. The island is only accessible at low tide, so the two daily tours depart at different times each day (check with the St. Andrews Welcome Centre for

times). You will be asked to meet at the end of Bar Road, two kilometers northeast of town, from where you follow a lead vehicle across a strip of sand that is exposed only at low tide. The entry fee includes a guided tour.

Huntsman Aquarium

Beyond the golf course, Huntsman Aquarium (Brandy Cove Rd., 506/529-1202; mid-May–Aug. daily 10 A.M.–6 P.M., Sept. Thurs.–Sun. 10 A.M.–5 P.M.; adult $14, senior $11.50, child $9.50) is part of the Huntsman Marine Science Centre, a nonprofit marine-biology study facility drawing researchers from far and wide. The aquarium is stocked with hundreds of local fish, crustaceans, mollusks, and marine plant species. A touch tank gives children gentle access to intertidal critters, while seals cavort in the outdoor pool. The center also offers environmental classes with guest lecturers and field/lab work (around $1,000 per week).

Atlantic Salmon Interpretive Centre

On the road back to Saint John, the Atlantic Salmon Interpretive Centre (Chamcook Lake Rd., 506/529-1384; mid-May–mid-Oct. daily 9 A.M.–5 P.M.; adult $6, child $4) is part of a much larger research facility. Displays describe the life cycle of Atlantic salmon and breeding techniques. From the sun-filled room, paths lead upstream to Chamcook Lake and downstream to Passamaquoddy Bay.

SHOPPING

Craft and gift shops abound. Whether you're looking for sweaters, souvenir T-shirts, locally produced pottery, or what have you, one of the de rigueur activities in St. Andrews is strolling along Water Street and drifting in and out of the shops. One of the nicest is **Boutique la Baleine** (173 Water St., 506/529-3926).

RECREATION
On the Water

Whale-watching is a popular activity here, and several companies offer cruises in search of finback, minke, and humpback whales. In

Whale-watching is a popular activity in St. Andrews.

drawn to the scenic fairways of the **Fairmont Algonquin Golf Course** (Brandy Cove Rd., 506/529-8165) for more than 100 years. The course was thoroughly modernized in 2000, with a complete redesign that highlights the sparkling Bay of Fundy at every turn. Summer greens fees are $99, with discounts early and late in the season. Rates include access to the driving range and a power cart.

ACCOMMODATIONS AND CAMPING

St. Andrews has a wealth of options, ranging from the family-friendly (Seaside Beach Resort) to the extravagant (take your pick). Always make reservations for July and August.

$50-100

A couple of inexpensive but clean and comfortable motels are along the road into town, including the **Picket Fence Motel** (102 Reed Ave., 506/529-8985, www.picketfencenb.com; $75–95 s or d), where the pricier units have basic cooking facilities.

$100-150

For inexpensive no-frills waterfront accommodations, it's difficult to recommend anywhere but **C Seaside Beach Resort** (339 Water St., 506/529-3846 or 800/506-8677, www.seaside.nb.ca; $90–220). Within walking distance of downtown, this complex comprises a collection of buildings dating back to the mid-1800s. There are 24 units, some of which are self-contained cabins; others are larger structures complete with slanted floors and handmade windows. My favorite is Harbourview Two, which is right on the water and has two bedrooms and a small deck with a barbecue. All units have kitchens and older televisions.

Garden Gate Bed and Breakfast (364 Montague St., 506/529-4453, www.bbgardengate.com; $90–130 s or d) is a lovely late-19th-century home surrounded by mature gardens. Each of the four rooms has an en suite or private bathroom, and rates include a cooked breakfast.

addition to whales, you'll see harbor seals and lots of seabirds. All tours depart from the wharf at the foot of King Street.

Quoddy Link Marine (6 King St., 506/529-2600) has a stable covered boat that takes visitors on three-hour naturalist-narrated cruises. Light snacks and beverages and the use of binoculars and foul-weather gear are included in the price (adult $60, senior $54, child $34). For the more adventurous, **Fundy Tide Runners** (16 King St., 506/529-4481) runs out to the whale-watching area in large inflatable Zodiacs for a similar price.

Eastern Outdoors (165 Water St., 506/529-4662) offers a three-hour paddle around Passamaquoddy Bay from the St. Andrews waterfront, with an emphasis on wildlife and human history. The cost is a reasonable $49 per person.

Golf

St. Andrews may not have the history of its Scottish namesake, but golfers have been

Views from the sweeping lawns of **Rossmount Inn** (4599 Hwy. 127, 506/529-3351 or 877/529-3351, www.rossmountinn.com; Apr.–Dec.; $115–138 s or d) extend unimpeded across Passamaquoddy Bay. The three-story mansion holds a dining room, a lounge, an outdoor pool, and 18 guest rooms decorated in soothing cream colors and furnished with Victorian antiques. Outdoors, guests congregate on the patio or use the walking trails to explore the expansive 35-hectare grounds. The lodge is six kilometers northeast of town.

$150-200

Right on the edge of the bay and 200 meters from the heart of the village, **St. Andrews Motor Inn** (111 Water St., 506/529-4571, www.standrewsmotorinn.com; $160–230 s or d) is a modern three-story motel. The rates are high for a reason—most rooms have balconies with magnificent water views.

Over $200

The Tudor-style **Fairmont Algonquin** (184 Adolphus St., 506/529-8823 or 800/257-7544, www.fairmont.com; from $320 s or d) is a classy Canadian resort, with manicured grounds dominating the hill above St. Andrews. Everything about it bespeaks gentility and class—verdant lawns dotted with flowerbeds, gardens, young couples in tennis whites leisurely sipping cool drinks on the veranda—and the tinkling of crystal is the loudest noise you'll hear in the formal dining room. Within, the public and guest rooms are arrayed with overstuffed furniture, Oriental rugs, and gleaming dark furniture. The resort's image is very proper, and so are the members of the staff, who are snappily attired in Scottish ceremonial garb, replete with kilts. Amenities include multiple dining rooms, a lounge, an outdoor pool, tennis courts, a health spa, and squash/racquetball courts.

A member of the prestigious Relais & Chateaux group, the **Kingsbrae Arms** (219 King St., 506/529-1897, www.kingsbrae.com; $395–795 s or d) features eight of the most luxurious guest rooms you'll find anywhere in Atlantic Canada. From the marble bathrooms to the refined room service, this is the place for a serious splurge.

© ANDREW HEMPSTEAD

The large deck at Seaside Beach Resort is the perfect place to relax with a morning coffee.

Campground

Through town to the east, and a 10-minute walk to downtown, **C Kiwanis Oceanfront Camping** (Indian Point Rd., 506/529-3439, www.kiwanisoceanfrontcamping.com; early Apr.–Oct.; $31–38) lives up to its name, with a front row of campsites that enjoy unimpeded water views. Amenities include showers, a playground, a grocery store, a kitchen shelter, wireless Internet access, and a laundry.

FOOD

While St. Andrews has cafés and restaurants to suit all tastes and budgets, seafood dominates local menus.

Cafés

Locals head to places like **Sweet Harvest Market** (182 Water St., 506/529-6249; daily from 8 A.M.) for European-style breads, oversized cinnamon buns, and the daily muffin special.

As you continue east along the waterfront, **Market Square Grill** (211 Water St., 506/529-8241) has a coffee counter serving gourmet sandwiches made to order and hot drinks (daily 8 A.M.–7 P.M.) and a more substantial restaurant facing the town square (daily 11 A.M.–10 P.M.).

Restaurants

If you're after casual seafood dining with water views, look no farther than **C Gables Restaurant** (143 Water St., 506/529-3440; July–Aug. daily 8 A.M.–11 P.M., Sept.–May daily 11 A.M.–9 P.M.; $14–24), which occupies a choice spot right on the bay. The waterfront wooden deck out back is a great place for lunch, and couldn't be more romantic in the evening—a great spot for sipping an after-dinner cognac and watching the lights shimmer across the water. The menu stays the same for lunch and dinner, with blackboard specials your best bet. Last time I was through, the seafood pie was delicious. The entrance is down an alleyway (if you pass a massive lobster wood carving, you've found the right spot).

Also right on the water is the **Lighthouse Restaurant** (1 Patrick St., 506/529-3082; Wed.–Mon. 5–9 P.M.), on a small headland jutting into the ocean at the south end of town (you can see the adjacent lighthouse from downtown). It's a big room, with basic furnishings and a casual vibe. Favorites include grilled teriyaki salmon ($19) and baked haddock wrapped in thin slices of smoked salmon ($24), or you can order boiled lobster from $25.

You don't need to be a guest at the Fairmont Algonquin (184 Adolphus St., 506/529-8823) to take advantage of its various eating options, including **The Veranda** (May–Oct. daily 6:30 A.M.–9:30 P.M.; $17–32), which specializes in modern presentations of regional game and produce. The resort's **Library Lounge** (daily 5–9 P.M.; $21–35) is a casual yet elegant restaurant that opens to the terrace.

INFORMATION

As you enter town from the west, the **St. Andrews Visitor Information Centre** (24 Reed Ave., 506/529-3556, www.standrewsbythesea.ca; early May–early Oct. daily 9 A.M.–6 P.M.) is tucked away in the trees on the left side of the road beyond the Picket Fence Motel.

Fundy Isles

The Fundy Isles are a world away from mainland living, an archipelago of islands spread across the New Brunswick side of the Bay of Fundy. Four islands—Deer, Campobello, Grand Manan, and White Head—are populated and are linked to the mainland by ferry. They make an interesting diversion from coastal cruising and are little known outside Atlantic Canada.

DEER ISLAND

The sea swirls mightily around Grand Manan but diminishes in intensity as the currents spin off around the coast of Maine to Deer Island, which lies closer to the United States than the Canadian mainland. Sovereignty of Deer and Campobello Islands was disputed for decades after the American Revolution; a treaty gave the islands to New Brunswick in the 1840s.

Sights and Recreation

Wilder and with a lower profile than Campobello, Deer Island is nevertheless reached first from the New Brunswick mainland. It's devoted to fishing and is encircled with herring weirs (stabilized seine nets); other nets create the "world's largest lobster pounds." The **Old Sow,** the largest tidal whirlpool in the Western Hemisphere, can be viewed three hours before high tide from **Deer Island Point Park** at the island's south end.

Accommodations

A great place to stay is **◖ Sunset Beach Cottage & Suites** (21 Cedar Grove Rd., 506/747-2972, www.cottageandsuites. com; May–Sept.), which has an outdoor pool and a gazebo built right on the ocean. Accommodations are provided in five self-contained suites ($80 s or d) and one cottage ($840 per week), all with water views.

Getting There

Ferries to Deer Island depart year-round from Letete, 15 kilometers from Highway 1 (turn off at Exit 56, four kilometers west of St. George). Ferries depart up to 20 times daily from 7 A.M. The government-run service is free and no reservations are taken. Between late June and early September, Deer Island is linked by ferry to Eastport (Maine) by **East Coast Ferries** (506/747-2159, www.eastcoastferriesltd.com). Departures are hourly in each direction, and the cost is $16 per vehicle and driver plus $3 for each extra passenger.

CAMPOBELLO ISLAND

Linked by a bridge to Lubec, Maine, Campobello is inextricably linked to the United States, but in summer a ferry links the island to Deer Island, making it a natural extension of your travels through the Fundy Isles.

Campobello, cloaked in granite, slate, and sandstone, was a favorite retreat of U.S. president Franklin Delano Roosevelt. The shingled green and bell-pepper-red family vacation home is now the main attraction at the **Roosevelt Campobello International Park** (Hwy. 774, Welshpool, 506/752-2922; late May–early Oct. daily 10 A.M.–6 P.M.; free). The 34-room interior is furnished with authentic family trappings, made somehow all the more poignant because FDR was stricken with polio while on vacation here.

Parks

East-facing 425-hectare **Herring Cove Provincial Park** (506/752-7010; May–mid-Oct.) has a long stretch of beach, six hiking trails, and a nine-hole golf course (506/752-7041; greens fees $26). Around half of the campground's sites come with electricity, and all have picnic tables and fire pits.

Getting There

Aside from driving to the island from Maine, between late June and mid-September you can reach Campobello by ferry from Deer Island. **East Coast Ferries** (506/747-2159, www.eastcoastferriesltd.com) schedules hourly crossings

9 A.M.–6 P.M. The fare for vehicle and driver is $16, plus $3 per passenger.

GRAND MANAN ISLAND

As the Fundy Isles' largest and most southerly island, Grand Manan (pop. 2,700) gets the brunt of the mighty Fundy high tide. Pity the centuries of ships that have been caught in the currents during malevolent storms; near the island, shipwrecks litter the seafloor and pay homage to the tide's merciless power. Four lighthouses atop the island's lofty headland ceaselessly illuminate the sea lanes and warn ships off the island's shoals.

Apart from the surging tide, Grand Manan is blissfully peaceful. White, pink, and purple lupines and dusty pink wild roses nod with the summer breezes. Windswept spruce, fir, and birch shade the woodland pockets. Amethyst and agate are mixed with pebbles on the beaches at **Whale Cove, Red Point,** and **White Head Island** offshore. Dulse, a nutritious purple seaweed rich in iodine and iron, washes in at **Dark Harbour** on the western coast, and islanders dry and package the briny snack for worldwide consumption.

Offshore, every species of marine life known to the Bay of Fundy congregates in the bay's nutrient-rich mouth. Whales in pursuit of herring schools swim in on incoming currents—the right, finback, humpback, and minke whales cavort in the tempestuous seas. They're at their most numerous when the plankton blooms, mid-July through September.

Bird-Watching

Birds of almost 350 species flutter everywhere in season, and each species has a place on this rock in the sea. Seabirds and waterfowl nest at the **Castalia Marsh** on the island's eastern side. Ducks and geese by the thousands inhabit the **Anchorage Beach** area, where a wet-heath bird sanctuary is speckled with ponds. Expect to see bald eagles and other raptors on the southern cliffs from mid-August through November. The eider, storm petrel, and Atlantic puffin prefer offshore islets.

Bird populations are thickest from early April through June and late summer to autumn. A great way to see the birds is by hiking one of the 18 trails (totaling 70 kilometers) that crisscross the headland. Many wind through bird sanctuaries. Another incredible place for bird-watching is **Machias Seal Island,** the outermost bird sanctuary island. Boat tours, restricted to a limited number of passengers, depart Grand Manan to see the archipelago's highest concentration of exotic bird species, including razorbill auks, arctic terns, and 900 pairs of nesting Atlantic puffins.

Tours

While you can take whale- and bird-watching trips from St. Andrews, Grand Manan is where serious nature lovers base themselves. Space is limited and is always in demand on the following tours, so make reservations.

One of the finest, most well-established sightseeing outfits in town is **Sea Watch Tours** (North Head, 506/662-8552, www.seawatchtours.com), which runs tour boats ($90 for a six-hour trip) to Machias Seal Island late June–early August. Whale-watching tours are scheduled July–September and cost around $65.

Accommodations and Camping

Though lodgings can be found across the island, it's smart to book ahead. **Compass Rose** (65 Route 776, North Head, 506/662-8570, www.compassroseinn.com; May–Oct.; $89–129 s, $99–139 d) sits atop a headland on the edge of North Head. Its six comfortable guest rooms are spread through two buildings, one of which was the island's original post office. Breakfast is served in a sunny dining room, and seafood-oriented lunches are offered through the summer season.

Shorecrest Lodge (100 Route 776, North Head, 506/662-3216, www.shorecrestlodge.com; mid-May–mid-Nov.; $90–120 s or d) is a favorite with the bird-watching crowd (especially the late August through September migratory pelagic bird season). The 10 rooms in this historic inn each have private bathrooms and frilly fabrics and wallpaper, while other amenities include a TV room, a veranda with water views, a library filled with field guides, and a restaurant open for dinner with advance reservations. A continental breakfast is included in the rates.

You'll need a vehicle to get to **Anchorage Provincial Park** (Seal Cove, 506/662-7022; May–Oct.), at the south end of the island. The park contains 100 unserviced ($28) or serviced ($32) campsites with toilets, hot showers, and kitchen shelters. Reservations are not accepted, so it's wise to call ahead to check on availability.

Food

For a quick pizza or burger, try **Fundy House Takeout** (1303 Route 776, Grand Manan, 506/662-8341; summer daily 9 A.M.–11 P.M.; $8–14). **North Head Bakery** (199 Route 776, North Head, 506/662-8862; Tues.–Sat. 6 A.M.–6 P.M.) has a great selection of cookies and cakes, plus bread baked daily from organic ingredients.

Getting There

Coastal Transport Ltd. (506/642-0520, www.coastaltransport.ca) operates a ferry line between Blacks Harbour (11 kilometers south of Exit 60 from Highway 1) and North Head. The 27-kilometer crossing takes about 90 minutes. The car/passenger ferries sail daily year-round, with up to seven departures scheduled daily July to early September. The round-trip fare (adult $10.90, child $5.40, vehicle from $32.55) is collected when leaving the island. Reservations are not taken for travel to the island, so plan on arriving at least one hour prior to departure. Reservations *are* taken for the return journey, so call ahead to be sure of a spot, especially in July and August.

Upper Fundy Coast

The impact of tidal action is extraordinarily dramatic on the Upper Fundy's coastline. The sea floods into the bay and piles up on itself, ravaging the shore at Mispec—where it has clawed into the land's edge to reveal gold veins—and pocking the coastline with spectacular caves at St. Martins. St. Martins also marks the starting point for the region's most challenging trek—to Fundy National Park. The backpacking trip involves just 40 kilometers, but expect to spend 3–5 days. In places the high tide washes out all beach access and forces hikers back inland.

Beyond the national park, the tide's strength increases as the bay forks into the narrow Chignecto Bay and Cumberland Basin. No place is safe during an incoming tide, especially the stretch of coast from Saint John to Hopewell Cape. At Alma, the village at the park's eastern edge, the sea rises waist-high in a half hour and continues rising to a height of 14 meters.

The Fundy orchestrates its final swan song at Hopewell Cape. Beyond the cape, its tidal impact is exhausted; some of the sea moves inland as a tidal bore and flows up the Petitcodiac River to Moncton, and the remainder washes Dorchester Peninsula's coastal marsh edges.

SAINT JOHN TO FUNDY NATIONAL PARK

From Saint John, it's 55 kilometers northeast along Highway 1 to Exit 211, from which the boundary of Fundy National Park is 22 kilometers southeast. This inland route misses St. Martins, a delightful old shipbuilding port reached from Saint John by following Highway 111 east from the airport.

St. Martins

St. Martins, founded in 1783 as Quaco, became one of the busiest shipbuilding centers in the Maritimes in the 1800s, turning out more than 500 ships over the course of the 19th century. Today the handsome little village is a fishing port, as evidenced by the stacks of lobster

FUNDY BIRDING

In the Upper Fundy, where the tides are at their most dramatic, the setting belongs to a few remote villages and one of North America's most spectacular shows of migratory birds. The American bittern, Virginia rail, short-eared owl, marsh wren, and hundreds of other species soar across the wide stage. The bird-watching season varies according to species, but it generally runs late March to late May and August through September.

One of the best bird-watching spots is **Grand Manan Island**. On the mainland, bird sanctuaries are scattered from upper Chignecto Bay's western coast across Shepody Bay to the Dorchester Peninsula and the Chignecto Isthmus. They are easily missed – signs are often obscure, and numbered roads may be the only landmarks. Many are managed by **Ducks Unlimited Canada** (506/458-8848), a nonprofit environmental group that manages around 20,000 hectares of wetlands in New Brunswick alone. Another good source of information is the **Canadian Wildlife Service,** which has its Atlantic head office at **Sackville Waterfowl Park** (17 Waterfowl Ln., Sackville, 506/364-5044; Mon.-Fri. 8 A.M.-4 P.M.). At this location, there is a display room with details of species you're likely to spot in the adjacent wetland as well as down the road at the **Tintamarre Sanctuary,** a national wildlife area. A similar reserve is **Shepody National Wildlife Area** between Alma and Hopewell Cape.

traps on the quay. At the harbor, two covered wooden bridges stand within a stone's throw of one another. The local tourist information office is housed in the lighthouse close by.

Some of the great attractions in the vicinity are the seaside caves scooped out of the red sandstone cliffs by the Fundy tides. The caves can be explored at low tide.

The village has two excellent accommodations, and being just a 40-minute drive from downtown Saint John, it's worth considering staying an extra night and using St. Martins as a base for a day trip to the city. The historic **Tidal Watch Inn** (16 Beach St., 506/833-4772 or 888/833-4772, www.tidalwatchinn.ca; $110–225 s or d) has comfortable beach house quarters with 15 guest rooms, a dining room open daily for dinner, and a hot tub housed outdoors in a gazebo. Overlooking the Bay of Fundy, the Victorian Gothic **C St. Martins Country Inn** (303 Main St., 506/833-4534 or 800/565-5257, www.stmartinscountryinn.com; $95–165 s or d), former home of one of the seaport's most prosperous shipbuilding families, has aptly been dubbed "the Castle" by locals. The beautifully restored mansion has 17 antique-furnished rooms, each with private bath and some with canopied beds.

C FUNDY NATIONAL PARK

This magnificent park is a bit out of the way but well worth the effort to get to. The 206-square-kilometer park encompasses a cross-section of Fundy environments and landforms: highlands; deeply cut valleys; swampy lowlands; dense forests of red and sugar maple, yellow birch, beech, red spruce, and balsam fir; and a shoreline of dizzying cliffs and sand and shingle beaches. For all its wilderness, though, Fundy National Park has a surprising number of civilized comforts, including rustic housekeeping chalets, a motel, a restaurant, and a golf course.

From Saint John, Highway 1 feeds into the TransCanada Highway, and the backcountry Highway 114 branches off east of Sussex, peels over the Caledonia Highlands, and plummets through woodlands to sea level. Thick woods rise on one side and conceal the park's deep valleys sown with rivers and waterfalls. Glimpses of the sea, cradled by beaches, appear on the road's other side; most of the 13-kilometer shoreline is wrapped with formidably steep sandstone cliffs.

Park Entry

The park is open year-round, though full services operate (and entry fees are charged) only from mid-May to mid-October. A one-day pass, valid until 4 P.M. the following day, is adult $8, senior $7, child $4.

Hiking

Two dozen hiking trails wander the coastline or reach up into the highlands. The highlands hikes are easy-to-moderate treks, while the toughest trails lie along the coast, impeded by cliffs, ridges, fern glades, and thick forests.

Shorter, easier trails include the **Caribou Plain,** a 3.4-kilometer loop on flat terrain through forest and bog, and **Dickson Falls,** a 1.5-kilometer loop that offers views above and below the waterfall via a system of boardwalks and stairs. The moderately difficult **Goose River Trail** is 7.9 kilometers each way, along an old cart track to a wilderness campground at the mouth of Goose River in the park's southwestern corner. The 10-kilometer (each way) **Coastal Trail** is graded as difficult, but the rewards include lush fern glades and forest and great ridge-top views over the bay and coastal sea stacks. You can get more detailed information at park headquarters or the Wolfe Lake information center, both of which sell the useful *Fundy National Park Trail Guide.*

Other Recreation

Beyond the grassed meadow below the Visitor Reception Centre is the **Saltwater Pool** (summer 11 A.M.–7 P.M.; adult $4, senior $3.50, child $2), which is filled with heated saltwater piped in from the Bay of Fundy. If you prefer to be on the water rather than in it, head to **Bennett Lake,** where canoe, kayak, and rowboat rentals are $10 per hour.

Fishing is good for the plentiful trout found in the lakes and rivers; a national park fishing license, available at either visitor center, is required ($10 per day; $35 for an annual pass valid in all national parks).

Fundy National Park Golf Course (506/887-2970; mid-May–mid-Oct.) is a fun, old-fashioned nine-hole layout that tumbles down the hillside near the administration building and slices through the coastal forest like a green velvet glove whose fingers reach into the woodlands. The greens fee is $19 for nine holes, or you can play all day for $35. Adjacent to the golf course are **tennis courts** and **lawn bowling;** rental equipment is available at the pro shop.

Accommodations

Lodging within the park and in the adjacent fishing village of **Alma** is well-priced. The best deal is at **Vista Ridge Cottages** (41 Foster Rd., 506/887-2808, www.fundyparkchalets. com; $99 s or d), which are within walking distance of most park attractions. Each cabin has three bedrooms, a small kitchen, an electric fireplace, and satellite TV.

Fundy Highlands Inn and Chalets (8714 Hwy. 114, 506/887-2930 or 888/883-8639, www.fundyhighlandchalets.com; $94–109 s or d) is two kilometers from the main facility area and enjoys a lofty location high above the bay in the Caledonia Highlands. Choose between comfortable rooms in the main lodge or chalets with water views. All units have cooking facilities.

Parkland Village Inn (8601 Main St., 506/887-2313 or 866/668-4337, www.parklandvillageinn.com; $95–150 s or d) is a 50-year-old three-story motel with a waterfront location along Alma's main street. The rooms are simple but modern, and most have water views. The two-bedroom suites are a steal at $150.

Campgrounds

The park has four campgrounds. Reservations can be made through the **Parks Canada Campground Reservation Service** (450/505-8302 or 877/737-3783, www.pccamping.ca) for $11 per booking, but they are only really necessary for weekends in July and August.

Headquarters Campground (late June–early Sept.; $26–36) is within walking distance of the Visitor Reception Centre, the swimming pool, the golf course, and Seawinds Dining

Room. Facilities include showers, playgrounds, and full hookups. Back up Highway 114 a little way is **Chignecto North Campground** (mid-May–mid-Oct.; $26–36), with similar facilities.

At the end of Point Wolfe Road, six kilometers southwest of the Visitor Reception Centre, ⚞ **Point Wolfe Campground** (late June–early Sept.; $26) has a delightful beachside location and is linked to coastal hiking trails. It has showers but no hookups.

In the park's northwest corner, **Wolfe Lake Campground** (mid-May–mid-Oct.; $16) has basic facilities such as pit toilets and fire pits.

Food
The only restaurant within the park is **Seawinds Dining Room** (506/887-2098; late May–mid-Oct. daily 11 A.M.–9:30 P.M.; $12–21), across from the Visitor Reception Centre beside the golf course. In all regards, it is a classically old-fashioned resort dining room, suited to families, well-priced, and with funky decorations that include three wrought-iron chandeliers, model ships, and the shell of a 13.5-pound lobster. Seafood dominates, with a lunchtime lobster roll and fries costing $12 and the dinner menu topping out at $21 for poached salmon covered with hollandaise sauce.

For locally harvested seafood to take back and cook at your campsite, head for ⚞ **Butland's** (8607 Main St., Alma, 506/887-2190, early May–early Sept. daily 10 A.M.–6 P.M., early Sept.–Dec. Sat.–Sun. noon–5 P.M.), which sells live and cooked lobsters, scallops, salmon, and haddock. Also in Alma is **Tides** (Parkland Village Inn, 8601 Main St., 506/887-2313; daily for breakfast, lunch, and dinner; $11–21), a casual dining room overlooking the Bay of Fundy.

Information
The main **Visitor Reception Centre** (506/887-6000, www.pc.gc.ca; spring and fall daily 8:30 A.M.–4:15 P.M., mid-June–early Sept. daily 8 A.M.–9:45 P.M., winter Mon.–Fri. 8:15 A.M.–4:30 P.M.) is on the park's eastern

edge, just across the river from the village of Alma. In addition to handing out general park information, the center is home to various natural history displays and holds a large bookstore.

Entering from the northwest, you'll find a small visitor center beside picturesque Wolfe Lake (Hwy. 114; late June–early Sept. daily 10 A.M.–5:45 P.M.).

ALMA TO HOPEWELL CAPE
It's 40 kilometers from Alma to Hopewell Cape, but for bird-watchers there is one important detour.

Shepody National Wildlife Area
Shepody National Wildlife Area—New Brunswick's stellar bird-watching sanctuary—is made up of three different habitat areas. **Germantown/Beaver Brook Marshes,** 14.7 kilometers northeast of Alma, is the reserve's only inland area and spreads out on 686 hectares on Highway 114's east side. As you approach the area, look for Midway Road, the reserve's southern boundary. Turn right on Midway, cross the covered bridge, and park beyond it at the second path. The nine-kilometer trail follows the marsh's edge alongside woodlands and fields rich with ducks and herons.

The 185-hectare **New Horton Marsh** attracts ducks and herons to a coastal setting. At Alma, take coastal Highway 915 for a 30-kilometer drive to the mudflats. The reserve's northern tip is situated where the road divides; one branch leads to inland Riverside-Albert, the other to Mary's Point Road farther out on the coast. A four-kilometer trek through the marsh starts on a dike off the latter road. *Be wary of the tides:* the mudflats reach almost to the sea and quickly flood.

A few kilometers beyond New Horton Marsh, Mary's Point Road leads to **Mary's Point,** Canada's only shorebird reserve. Shorebirds by the hundreds of thousands set down on the 109-hectare coastal reserve, their

At low tide, the boats in Alma Harbour end up on the drained ocean floor.

© ANDREW HEMPSTEAD

numbers peaking mid-July through mid-August. Among the onslaught are about 9,000 blue herons and an uncountable number of cormorants, all of which swarm over the intertidal zone.

HOPEWELL CAPE

The great Fundy tides have created a curiously compelling scene at Hopewell Cape, 40 kilometers northeast of Alma and 35 kilometers south of Moncton.

◖ Hopewell Rocks

Hopewell Cape is the place-name, and Hopewell Rocks (Hwy. 114, 506/734-3534; mid-May–mid-Oct. daily 9 A.M.–5 P.M., July–Aug. until 8 P.M.; adult $9, senior $8, child $7) is the name of the natural attraction. You pay the entry fee at the tollgate and then are directed to the main visitor center, where interesting displays describe the geology of the cape and its relationship to the Fundy tides.

Trails lead to a number of cliff-top lookouts,

but the vast majority of visitors make a beeline for the **Flowerpot Rocks.** The walking trail takes around 20 minutes, or you can pay $2 each way to ride the oversized golf cart shuttle. Either way, next up is a steep descent down a stairway to the ocean floor. At the staircase's first landing, you overlook an otherworldly collection of giant natural arches and mushroom-shaped pillars jutting up from the sea floor. Known as "flowerpots," these sea-sculpted red shale and conglomerate sea stacks have been separated from the mainland cliffs by the abrasive tide. Many of the flowerpots are "planted" with stunted black spruce and balsam fir, looking somewhat like clipped haircuts stuck atop the stacks. At low tide, sightseers—dwarfed by the enormous pillars—roam the beach and retrieve seashells left by the tide. Be wary of falling rocks; the pillars and cliffs are continually eroding, and there's always a chance that rocks will loosen and tumble.

It's only possible to "walk on the ocean floor" (as it's promoted) around the flowerpots from three hours before low tide to two hours after. Catch the scene again at high tide and you'll understand why. The tide rises 16 meters here, fully flooding the area. All you'll see are the pillars' tree-covered crowns. Information centers in Fundy National Park and Moncton will be able to tell you when the tide is low at Hopewell Rocks, or check the website, www. thehopewellrocks.ca. Be forewarned: When low tide falls during the middle of the day in July and August, the "ocean floor" gets *extremely* crowded.

Accommodations and Food

Near the access road is **Hopewell Rocks Motel** (Hwy. 114, 506/734-2975 or 888/759-7070, www.hopewellrocksmotel.com; $125 s or d, includes two passes to Hopewell Rocks), which has 33 rooms with water views, an outdoor swimming pool, and a restaurant with lots of seafood and dishes such as roast beef dinners under $15.

SAINT JOHN

© ANDREW HEMPSTEAD

The "flower pots" at Hopewell Rocks are New Brunswick's most distinctive geological feature.

SAINT JOHN RIVER VALLEY

The Saint John River originates in remote northern Maine near the Québec border and enters New Brunswick's northwestern corner alongside Highway 205, a backcountry road used more by loggers than sightseers. The young river tumbles along, over riverbed boulders and through glistening pools frequented by moose and white-tailed deer. It flows through Edmundston and then curves southeast through the French-flavored towns and villages of Madawaska until it's squeezed into a spuming torrent at the stony gorge at Grand Falls. The rest of the river's journey grows increasingly placid. It's tamed by hydro dams at Beechwood and Mactaquac, and it flows under the world's longest covered bridge at Hartland before draining into the Bay of Fundy at Saint John. That city is covered in the *Saint John and the Fundy Coast* chapter—here we concentrate on the river's interior course, which splits the inland provincial capital of Fredericton in two. This small, genteel city of just 51,000 is a sightseer's delight, with an appealing historic downtown core, riverfront walking paths, and tree-lined streets feeding back to quiet residential areas of historic homes with open porches, bay windows, and gardens of pearl-colored peonies and scarlet poppies.

PLANNING YOUR TIME

The vast majority of travelers who traverse the length of the Saint John River arrive overland through Québec and make this western part of New Brunswick their first taste of the Maritimes. If you've flown into Halifax and

© ANDREW HEMPSTEAD

HIGHLIGHTS

◖ Historic Garrison District: Filling two blocks of downtown Fredericton, this wide-open attraction lets visitors step back in time – while surprising them with quirky attractions including a 17-kilogram frog (page 45).

◖ Beaverbrook Art Gallery: Atlantic Canada's finest art gallery holds an impressive collection of Canadian work, as well as paintings by notables like Salvador Dalí (page 47).

◖ Christ Church Cathedral: In a land of grandiose churches, this is one of the most impressive. Come for summer music recitals, or simply wander through the gardens and crane your neck to search out the spire (page 47).

◖ Kings Landing Historical Settlement: Loyalist history comes alive at this outdoor museum that will easily fill a full day (page 54).

◖ Hartland Covered Bridge: The most memorable way to reach the quiet village of Hartland is by crossing the Saint John River via the world's longest covered bridge (page 55).

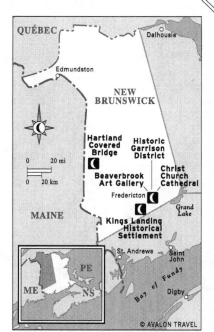

LOOK FOR ◖ TO FIND RECOMMENDED SIGHTS, ACTIVITIES, DINING, AND LODGING.

caught the ferry across the Bay of Fundy, it will take a little over an hour to reach Fredericton, which should be your focus for a day of sightseeing. This will give you enough time to explore the **Historic Garrison District,** walk through **Beaverbrook Art Gallery,** and marvel at **Christ Church Cathedral. Kings Landing Historical Settlement** is only a short drive from the capital, but it would make for a long day to lump it in with the other city attractions in a single day. Besides, you'll want to continue upriver to **Hartland** for the opportunity to drive across the world's longest covered bridge.

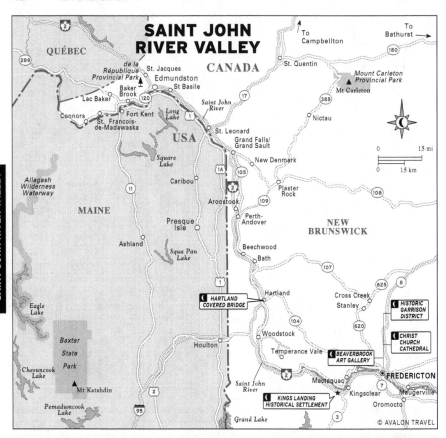

Fredericton and Vicinity

Fredericton (pop. 51,000), in the southwestern heart of the province, is New Brunswick's legislative, cultural, and educational center, and it's one of the country's oldest settlements. The city is the exception to the usual rule of thumb that a province's busiest and largest city is the logical choice for the capital. Fredericton is hardly a metropolis. Rather, it's of modest size, elegant, picture-book pretty, and very Anglo in tone and shape. "There is something subtle and elusive about it," Michael Collie wrote of Fredericton, "like a person who has had long sessions of psychoanalysis and has become more sophisticated and charming in the course of them."

Visitors flying in to New Brunswick will find Fredericton makes a good introduction to the province and a good sightseeing base. Roads lead from here to every part of the province. St. Andrews and Saint John on the Fundy are each just over an hour's drive south, and Moncton is 180 kilometers east. And it's always nice to return to Fredericton, the province's quintessential hometown.

© ANDREW HEMPSTEAD

Fredericton skyline

HISTORY

Fredericton is one of North America's oldest cities, though early attempts at settlement were short-lived. The French tried settlements in the late 1600s. Joseph Robineau de Villebon, Acadia's governor, built a fur-trading fort on the northern bank of the Saint John River at the mouth of the Nashwaak River. Heavy winter ice wrecked the fortification, and the inhabitants fled to Port-Royal across the Bay of Fundy. In 1713, the Treaty of Utrecht awarded mainland Nova Scotia to the British, and Acadians fled back across the Fundy and founded Saint-Anne's Point (now Fredericton's historic area). The British demolished the village after the Acadian deportation. Malecite people camped along what is now Woodstock Road but moved upriver to the Kingsclear area before the Loyalists arrived in the late 18th century.

The Capital's Fortuitous Beginning

The situation that made Fredericton provincial capital was an interesting one. After the American Revolution, Loyalists by the thousands poured into New Brunswick at Saint John. England directed the mass exodus from New York, but military forces at Saint John were unprepared for the onslaught.

Arriving Loyalists and families, finding limited food and no housing, rioted. Stung by the backlash, the British directed subsequent emigrants 103 kilometers upriver to Saint-Anne's Point. The Loyalists arrived in the wilderness, founded a new settlement as a "haven for the king's friends," and named it Frederick's Town in honor of King George III's second son. Two years later, in 1785, provincial governor Thomas Carleton designated the little river town the colonial capital, and the people of Saint John were permanently miffed.

England had great plans for Fredericton. Surveyor Charles Morris drew up the first street grid between University Avenue and Wilsey Road. By 1786 the population center had shifted, and central Fredericton as you see it today was redrawn by another surveyor and extended from riverfront to George Street, bounded by University Avenue and Smythe Street.

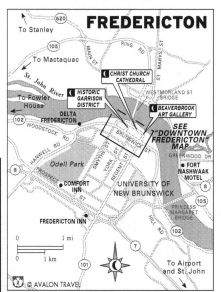

Priorities were established. Space was set aside for the Church of England sanctuary and King's College, now the University of New Brunswick. Public commons were marked off between the riverfront and Queen Street, except for two blocks earmarked for the British Army garrison.

The first winters were brutal, and Loyalists buried their dead at Salamanca on Waterloo Row. Wooden boardwalks were laid as sidewalks along muddy streets, and sewage was funneled into the river. The colonial government began at Government House in 1787, and New Brunswick's first assembly met the next year at a coffeehouse.

Expansion

The infamous Benedict Arnold lived awhile in Fredericton—and was burned in effigy at Saint John. Jonathan Odell, an influential Loyalist politician whose former estate land is now Odell Park, acted as negotiator between Arnold and England. American artist and naturalist John James Audubon visited Fredericton in 1830 and painted the *Pine*

Finch, one of his best-known works, during his stay at Government House.

By 1800, wharves lined the riverfront from Waterloo Row to Smythe Street, and sloops, schooners, and brigantines sped between the capital and Saint John. Shipping lumber was a profitable early business, and Fredericton added foundry products, processed leather, carriages, and wagons to its economy in the 1800s.

Fredericton and Christ Church Cathedral had a tightly woven beginning. The town was barely three generations old when Queen Victoria got wind of the cathedral's construction. But with fewer than 10,000 inhabitants, the settlement was hardly the proper setting for the first Anglican cathedral to be built on British soil since the Reformation. Royalty, of course, can do anything it wants, and Queen Victoria remedied the hitch. She elevated little Fredericton to the official "city" status required for an Anglican cathedral's setting. The city was incorporated in 1848, and in 1873 the city limits were extended to nearby towns, doubling the population. The city hall opened three years later.

Fires and Floods

Fredericton had its share of scourges. At various times, flames consumed even the sturdiest stone buildings, from Government House to the Military Compound's Guard House. Great conflagrations leveled 300 downtown buildings in 1849, destroyed 46 houses and stores in 1854, and took the first Christ Church Cathedral's steeple in 1911. Even the Westmoreland Street Bridge was vulnerable, and the first bridge, built in 1885, burned in 1905.

River floods were equally devastating: Queen Street was frequently under water during spring's ice melt. Floods in 1887 and 1923 swamped the capital. The upriver Mactaquac Dam was built to divert the river's impact, but floods again threatened the capital in 1973–1974.

The Town Evolves

England's plan for Fredericton as a miniature London was never fulfilled. Shipping and manufacturing diminished in the early 1900s, and Fredericton settled into a prosperous, genteel government town, university center, and haunt of the Anglo establishment. The **New Brunswick College of Craft and Design** started up in the 1940s and relocated to the renovated Military Compound in the 1980s. The **University of New Brunswick,** with 7,500 engineering, arts, education, business, and science students, overlooks the city from a steep hilltop and shares the campus with **St. Thomas University,** a Roman Catholic institution with 1,200 liberal arts students.

William Maxwell Aitken, better known as Lord Beaverbrook, paved the way for Fredericton's cultural accomplishments. The **Beaverbrook Art Gallery** was a gift to the city in 1959, and **Lord Beaverbrook Playhouse** across the street followed in 1964. It became the home of Theatre New Brunswick, Atlantic Canada's only provincial repertory touring company.

SIGHTS
◀ Historic Garrison District

This military compound (Queen St., 506/460-2129), a national historic site, dominates downtown, encompassing two long city blocks between the modern city to the south and the Saint John River to the north. Built in 1784 as headquarters for the British army, it is enclosed by a curlicue wrought-iron black fence that contains a variety of attractions.

At the corner of Queen and Carleton Streets, the stone **Officers' Quarters** was built in 1827. One street-level room is open to the public (July–Aug. daily 10 A.M.–6 P.M.; free), while around the back, low-ceilinged rooms once used to store ammunition now provide a home for vendors selling arts and crafts. Across the courtyard is the **Guard House,** a simple stone building (July–Aug. daily 10 A.M.–6 P.M.; free) that looks much like it would have in the mid-1800s, complete with costumed guards out front in summer.

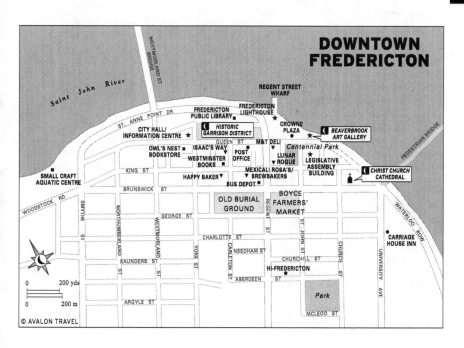

DOWNTOWN FREDERICTON

This wrought-iron arch forms the entranceway to the Historic Garrison District.

FREDERICTON REGION MUSEUM

Facing the Parade Square at the east end of the Historic Garrison District, this museum (517 Queen St., 506/455-6041; summer daily 10 A.M.–5 P.M.; adult $4, child $2) is housed within the former Officers' Quarters (1825), a three-story stone building unusually styled with a ground-level colonnade of white pillars and an iron handrail, designed by the Royal Engineers. The museum is devoted to provincial history from early Malecite and Mi'kmaq to contemporary events. The unlikely surprise is the Coleman Frog, a 17-kilogram, 1.6-meter-long amphibian stuffed for posterity and squatting inside a glass showcase on the second floor. The believe-it-or-not frog was found a century ago by local Fred Coleman, who developed a friendship with the frog and fattened it up by feeding it rum pudding and June bugs in honey sauce—or so the story goes.

SCHOOL DAYS MUSEUM

Step back into the classroom at the School Days Museum (corner of Queen and York Streets, 506/459-3738; early June–late Aug. Mon.–Fri. 10 A.M.–4 P.M., Sat. 1–4 P.M.; free), across York Street from City Hall. In addition to a reconstructed classroom, you'll find an interesting display on one-room schools, textbooks and training manuals, and furniture from as early as the mid-1800s.

NEW BRUNSWICK SPORTS HALL OF FAME

The John Thurston Clark Memorial Building is an impressive 1881 Second Empire French Revival edifice that once served as customs house and post office. The building now provides a home for the New Brunswick Sports Hall of Fame (503 Queen St., 506/453-3747; June–early Sept. Mon.–Fri. 8:30 A.M.–4 P.M.; adult $3, child $2), with exhibits highlighting the province's best sporting men and women.

City Hall

The red-brick city hall, at the corner of Queen and York Streets and across from the Historic Garrison District, is central to everywhere downtown. The elegant 1876 building has been city offices, a jail, a farmers market, and an opera house. Its high tower houses the city's copper clock, and the decorative fountain in front—crowned by the figurine that Frederictonians have dubbed "Freddie, the little nude dude"—was added in 1885.

Inside, the **Council Chamber** is adorned with a series of 27 locally produced tapestries depicting the city's history. The **Fredericton Visitors Bureau** (506/460-2129), in the building's front vestibule, conducts chamber tours (mid-May–early Oct. daily 8:15 A.M.–7:30 P.M.; the rest of the year by appointment weekdays 8:15 A.M.–4:30 P.M.).

Fredericton Lighthouse

Cross Regent Street from the Historic Garrison District to reach this privately operated lighthouse (615 Queen St., 506/460-2939; May–June Mon.–Fri. 10 A.M.–4 P.M. and Sat.–Sun. noon–4 P.M., July to early Sept.

daily 10 A.M.–9 P.M.; adult $2, child $1). The interior consists of 13 separate landings exhibiting shipping and river-sailing artifacts. The top level commands a magnificent riverfront view. At ground level, you'll find a gift shop, an outdoor café serving light lunches, and bike rentals.

◖ Beaverbrook Art Gallery

On the east side of downtown is Beaverbrook Art Gallery (703 Queen St., 506/458-0970; Mon.–Sat. 9 A.M.–5:30 P.M., Sun. noon–5:30 P.M.; adult $8, senior $6, child $3), which was donated to the city by New Brunswick art maven Lord Beaverbrook, also known as William Maxwell Aitken. The gallery boasts an impressive 2,000-piece collection—the most extensive British fine arts collection in Atlantic Canada, if not the nation. Among the British painters represented are Thomas Gainsborough, Sir Joshua Reynolds, John Constable, and Walter Richard Sickert. You'll find Graham Sutherland's sketches of Winston Churchill—drawn in preparation for Churchill's official portrait—and works by Atlantic Canada's Miller Brittain, Alex Colville, and Jack Humphrey. Also central to the collection are the oils of Cornelius Krieghoff, depicting social and domestic scenes of early life in Acadia. Lord Beaverbrook could not resist the European masters—Salvador Dalí's large-scale *Santiago El Grande* and Botticelli's *Resurrection* are prominently displayed.

Legislative Assembly Building

The splendidly regal legislative building (Queen St., 506/453-2527) lies kitty-corner from the gallery. The sandstone French Revival building spreads across a manicured lawn, its massive wings pierced with high arched windows, and the upper floor and tower rotunda are washed in glistening white. The building was completed in 1882 at a cost of $120,000, including construction and furnishings. The front portico entrance opens into an interior decorated in high Victorian style—the apex of expensive taste at the time. Glinting Waterford

prisms are set in brass chandeliers, and the spacious rooms are wallpapered in an Oriental design. The interior's pièce de résistance is the **Assembly Chamber,** centered around an ornate throne set on a dais and sheltered with a canopy.

John James Audubon's *Birds of America* is kept in the **Legislative Library.** One of four volumes is on display in a climate-controlled exhibit, and pages are periodically turned to show the meticulous paintings. Each of the building's nooks and corners has a story, which tour guides are eager to relate. Tours are offered through summer, daily 8:30 A.M.–6:30 P.M. Legislative sessions (Feb.–May and Oct.) are open to the public.

◖ Christ Church Cathedral

Gothic-styled cathedrals were designed to soar grandiosely toward heaven, and this storied stone cathedral is no exception. With a lofty copper-clad central spire and elegant linear stone tracery, the cathedral rises from a grassy city block at Church and Brunswick Streets (506/450-8500). Begun in 1845 and consecrated in 1853, this was the first entirely new cathedral founded on British soil since the Norman Conquest way back in 1066. It was rebuilt after a fire in 1911 and is still the place where the city's nabobs go to pay their respects to the benevolent powers that be. It's open year-round, with recitals taking place in summer Friday 12:10–12:50 P.M.

Historic Cemeteries

The **Old Burial Ground** is bounded by Regent, Brunswick, George, and Sunbury Streets. The site—spliced with walkways beneath tall trees—is one of two historic burial grounds in town. This spread of greenery was the final resting place for Loyalist notables.

The **Loyalist Cemetery** (formerly the Salamanca graveyard), on an unmarked gravel road off Waterloo Row at riverfront, is simpler and marks the final resting place of the founding Loyalists who died in that first winter of 1783–1784.

BY ANY OTHER NAME

Fredericton is known by many names. New Brunswickers have dubbed the city "North America's Last Surviving Hometown." You could debate the claim, perhaps, but it nonetheless does sum up local priorities.

The naming trend goes back to the 1800s, when locals ruefully joked that the city had a fire every Saturday night and dubbed it the "City of Fires." In 1911, one such fire destroyed the Christ Church Cathedral. The sanctuary was quickly rebuilt, its grandiose silhouette on the skyline leading to the moniker "Cathedral City."

Another Fredericton nickname, "City of Stately Elms," is a testament to Fredericton's leafy ambience. The quiet streets are lined mainly with elms, a choice that goes back to founding Loyalist times. They've survived centuries, even beating Dutch elm disease, which the city quelled in the 1960s and 1970s.

Fredericton's reputation as "Canada's Poets' Corner" is a tribute to native sons Bliss Carmen, Sir Charles G. D. Roberts, and Francis Joseph Sherman. And finally, the nickname "Canada's Pewtersmith Capital" singles out the city's preeminent craft, developed here first by pewtersmith Ivan Crowell in the 18th century.

© ANDREW HEMPSTEAD

Christ Church Cathedral

Odell Park

Of the 355 hectares of lush parkland throughout the city, Odell Park (Smythe St., 506/460-2038) is the choice spread, holding 16 kilometers of trails, formal lawns, duck ponds, a deer pen, barbecue pits, and picnic tables. The park is Fredericton's largest, covering 175 hectares (388 acres). It is best known for an arboretum holding every tree species in the province; a 2.8-kilometer walking trail divided into three loops wanders through the shady expanse.

RECREATION

The riverfront **Small Craft Aquatic Centre** (Woodstock Rd., 506/460-2260; July–Aug. daily 6:30–9 A.M. and noon–8:30 P.M., shorter hours in spring and fall) rents recreational rowing shells, canoes, and kayaks; gives lessons; and leads kayak tours.

ENTERTAINMENT AND EVENTS
Performing Arts

Fredericton specializes in entertaining summertime visitors. Outdoor festivities center around the Garrison Historic District, where **Theatre-in-the-Park** takes to the boards July to early September. Their humorous and historical productions take place Monday–Friday at 12:15 P.M. and on weekends at 2 P.M. In summer, musicians—pipe bands and folk, country, and bluegrass groups—perform outdoors in Officers' Square every Tuesday and Thursday at 7:30 P.M., in front of the Guard House on Wednesday at 12:30 P.M., and in the Main Street Amphitheatre Wednesday at 7 P.M. Classic movies are screened outdoors every Sunday at 9 P.M. Storytellers weave local history into interesting yarns every Wednesday at 3 P.M. in Barracks Square. Best of all, this entire program is presented free of charge.

Theatre New Brunswick, the province's only professional English-speaking theater company, operates full-tilt during the autumn-to-spring theater season at **The Playhouse Fredericton** (686 Queen St., 506/458-8344).

Pubs and Nightlife

Locals love their low-key pubs, and you will find many around the downtown core. The **Lunar Rogue** (625 King St., 506/450-2065) heads the list with English pub ambience, Canadian and British draft beer, and live music—usually with a Celtic flavor—several nights a week. A cluster of pubs surrounds Pipers Lane, an alley that connects the 300 blocks of King and Queen Streets. **Dolan's Pub** (349 King St., 506/454-7474) offers an excellent menu of pub grub and slightly fancier fare, as well as Beamish on tap and live entertainment Thursday–Saturday.

Touring rock groups head for **iRock** (339 King St., 506/444-0121), where the cover charge is $8–25. Featuring five bars and two dance floors, the venue presents pulsating high-energy rock Thursday–Saturday. This is as hip as it gets in Fredericton.

Festivals and Events

Festival Francophone, for three days late in May, celebrates Acadian language and culture with concerts, dancing, and children's activities. The festivities take place at Centre Communautaire Sainte-Anne (715 Priestman St., 506/453-2731).

The **New Brunswick Highland Games** (506/452-9244, www.highlandgames.ca), a three-day Celtic tribute featuring pipe bands, highland dancing, Gaelic singing, heavy sports, clan booths, and more, takes over the city the last weekend of July.

New Brunswick Day, the first Monday in August, brings parades, street-food vendors, and fireworks to the Historic Garrison District.

Fredericton had its first fall fair in 1825, and the tradition continues at the **Fredericton Exhibition** (506/458-8819, www.frex.ca), with six days of country fair trappings, including harness racing and stage shows, at the Fredericton Exhibition Grounds during early September.

The summer season finishes in a clamor of music, as the outdoor **Harvest Jazz and Blues Festival** (506/454-2583, www.harvestjazzandblues.com) takes over the downtown streets for five days in mid-September. It's billed as the biggest jazz and blues fest east of Montréal, and it features musicians from all over North America.

SHOPPING

Shopping areas are concentrated downtown, mainly along Regent, Queen, York, and King Streets, and the adjacent side streets, plus on Woodstock Road and at the malls.

Arts and Crafts

Several shops are known for craft specialties. **Aitkens Pewter** (408 Queen St., 506/453-9474) stocks handcrafted pewter hollowware, jewelry, and decorative pieces. **Cultures Boutique** (383 Mazzuca's Ln., 506/462-3088) is a nonprofit operation featuring crafts produced by third world artisans. It is off York Street between King and Queen Streets.

Gallery Connexion (440 York St., 506/454-1433) is a nonprofit artists' outlet with an eminent reputation for the province's arts. In a stylishly renovated residence, **Gallery 78** (796 Queen St., 506/454-5192; closed Mon.) is the oldest commercial art gallery in New Brunswick and stocks a collection of art from all over Canada.

ACCOMMODATIONS AND CAMPING

In keeping with its status as a provincial capital, Fredericton has a choice of downtown chain hotels, each offering a wide range of modern services aimed at business travelers. Other options are historic inns dotted around the outskirts of downtown and regular motels along major arteries. The main concentration of the latter is three kilometers south of downtown at the junction of Regent and Prospect Streets (Exits 6A and 6B of Hwy. 8).

Under $50

HI-Fredericton (621 Churchill Row, 506/450-4417, www.hihostels.ca; dorms $25–30, $35–40 s, $40–45 d), an affiliate of Hostelling International, is a restored heritage home five blocks south of the Historic Garrison District. Amenities include a kitchen, laundry, and living area. Guest rooms have a maximum of three beds, with most having just one or two. Check-in is 7 A.M.–noon and 6–10 P.M.

$50-100

Across the river from downtown, the **Fort Nashwaak Motel** (15 Riverside Dr., 506/472-4411 or 800/684-8999, www.fortnashwaak.com; from $75 s, $85 d) and, four kilometers downstream, the **Norfolk Motel** (815 Riverside Dr., 506/472-3278 or 800/686-8555, www.norfolkmotel.ca; $80 s, $85 d) are basic cheapies.

$100-150

The three-story Queen Anne Revival **Carriage House Inn** (230 University Ave., 506/452-9924 or 800/267-6068, www.carriagehouse-inn.net; $105 s, $115 d) is a restored three-story 1875 home southeast of downtown but still within walking distance. The 10 guest rooms are furnished with antiques; guests have use of a solarium and laundry. Breakfasts are a real treat.

None of the motels around the junction of Regent and Prospect Streets offer anything extraordinary. Instead, you get the reliability of chains such as the **Comfort Inn** (797 Prospect St., 506/453-0800 or 800/228-5150, www.choicehotels.ca; $105 s, $115 d). In the vicinity and one of the largest motels in the city is the four-story **Fredericton Inn** (1315 Regent St., 506/455-1430 or 800/561-8777, www.frederictoninn.nb.ca; $125 s or d), between

the Regent and Fredericton shopping malls. It has 200 guest rooms, two restaurants (one specializing in buffets), a lounge, and an indoor pool.

Around 20 kilometers west of downtown along Highway 102 (at Exit 274), **Riverside Resort** (35 Mactaquac Rd., 506/363-5111 or 800/561-5111, www.holidayfredericton.com; from $145 s or d) has a very un-city-like location within striking distance of Kings Landing. It's a sprawling property with a restaurant and lounge and a health center with a heated indoor pool, a hot tub, and an exercise deck. Six two-bedroom chalets ($280 s or d) are also on the manicured grounds.

❰ On the Pond (Rte. 615, Mactaquac, 506/363-3420 or 800/984-2555, www.onthepond.com; from $165 s or d) is a luxurious country inn where the emphasis is on being pampered in a back-to-nature environment. Guests enjoy a wide variety of spa services, proximity to Mactaquac Provincial Park and its golf course, and a fitness center. The eight guest rooms have an earthy old-world charm, with little niceties such as plush robes and inviting living areas. Bed-and-breakfast rates start at $160 per person, but check the website for spa and golf packages.

$150-200

Along the river, within striking distance of downtown attractions, is the **❰ Delta Fredericton** (225 Woodstock Rd., 506/457-7000 or 888/890-3222, www.deltahotels.com; from $199 s or d), which has an agreeable resort-style atmosphere centering on a large outdoor pool complex, complete with resort furniture and a poolside bar. It also has an indoor pool, a fitness room, two restaurants, and a lounge. Check the Delta website for discounted rooms, and maybe consider a splurge on a suite that will cost the same as a regular room in a big-city hotel.

Over $200

One of Fredericton's better lodgings is the **Crowne Plaza Fredericton Lord Beaverbrook** (659 Queen St., 506/455-3371 or 866/444-1946, www.cpfredericton.com; $210–440 s or d), aimed squarely at those in town on government business. Don't let the dowdy exterior of this bulky hotel put you off—a massive revamp modernized the 165 guest rooms. Amenities include an indoor pool and fitness complex, two dining rooms, and a lounge.

Campgrounds

The closest camping to Fredericton is at **Hartt Island RV Resort,** seven kilometers west of town on the TransCanada Highway (506/462-9400, www.harttisland.com; May–Oct.; $28–38), which is a great spot to enjoy river sports like canoeing and kayaking.

On the same side of the city, but on the north side of the river, **Mactaquac Provincial Park Campground** (Hwy. 105, 506/363-4747; mid-May–mid-Oct.; $25–29) is a huge facility 24 kilometers from downtown. In addition to 305 campsites, there's a golf course, hiking, biking, swimming, and fishing.

FOOD

Fredericton has a reputation for so-so dining. Don't believe it. True, you won't find tony dining rooms by the dozens, and aside from at a few fine restaurants, the cooking is less than fancy. Nonetheless, you can sample virtually all the capital's fare without a qualm, and your dining dollar will go a long way, too.

Cafés and Cheap Eats

If you're planning a picnic, **M & T Deli** (602 Queen St., 506/458-9068; Mon.–Fri. 7:30 A.M.–4 P.M.) does an admirable job of sourcing big city delicacies, such as New York-style bagels and Montréal smoked meats. Daily specials are well priced (it was shepherd's pie and salad for $6 when I stopped by).

(Happy Baker** (520 King St., 506/454-7200; Mon.–Fri. 7:30 A.M.–5:30 P.M., Sat. 8 A.M.–4 P.M.) is worth searching out in the bowels of the Carleton Plaza high-rise. In addition to the usual array of coffee concoctions, you can order bakery treats and full meals like maple curry chicken penne for around $10.

Year-round **Boyce Farmers' Market** (665

George St., between Regent St. and Saint John St., 506/451-1815; Sat. 6 A.M.–1 P.M.) lures *everybody* with stalls heaped with baked goods, homemade German sausage, other local delicacies, and crafts.

Pubs and Restaurants

The **Lunar Rogue** (625 King St., 506/450-2065; Mon.–Fri. 9 A.M.–1 A.M., Sat. 10 A.M.–1 A.M., Sun. 11 A.M.–10 P.M.; $11–23), one of Fredericton's most popular pubs, offers dining indoors or alfresco. The breakfasts are cheap and filling, and the Rogue serves lunches and worthy light dinners (Cornish pasties, stir-fry chicken, sirloin strip, and pub-grub specials such as barbecued chicken wings) as well.

Across the street and a block down, **Mexicali Rosa's** (546 King St., 506/451-0686; daily for lunch and dinner; $11–18) is part of an eastern Canadian chain of colorful Mexican restaurants. Expect all the usual Americanized food at reasonable prices. It's a long way from Mexico, but the recipes nonetheless come off quite well. Margaritas and cold *cerveza* are available. Anyone hankering for pizza can step next door to **BrewBakers** (546 King St., 506/459-0067; Mon.–Thurs. 11:30 A.M.–10 P.M., Fri. 11:30 A.M.–11 P.M., Sat. 5–11 P.M., Sun. 5–9 P.M.; $15–29), where the pizzas are baked in a wood-fired oven and accompanied by pastas and salads in a contemporary setting.

Enthusiastic local owners, a funky ambience, and well-priced meals make **(** Isaac's Way** (73 Carleton St., 506/472-7937; Mon.–Fri. 11 A.M.–11 P.M., Sat. 5–11 P.M., Sun. 5–9 P.M.; $15–18) a solid choice for lunch or dinner. Sample mains include nut-crusted steelhead trout and chicken breast roasted in a sweet ginger bourbon sauce.

Hotel Dining

The dining rooms at the major hotels are good bets for fancier fare. At the Crowne Plaza (659 Queen St., 506/451-1804), the **Terrace Room** (daily for breakfast, lunch, and dinner; $17–31), with city and river views, offers breakfast and lunch at moderate prices and dinner items using regional produce. The adjacent ⟨ **Governor's Room** (dinner only, mains $26–36) serves a more upscale menu of French fare and nouvelle cuisine.

At the Delta Fredericton, **Bruno's** (225 Woodstock Rd., 506/457-7000; Mon.–Fri. 6 A.M.–2 P.M. and 5–9 P.M., Sat. 7 A.M.–2 P.M. and 5–9 P.M., Sun. 7 A.M.–2 P.M.; $15–36) lures crowds for fare such as chicken saltimbocca— a sautéed stuffed chicken breast basted with white wine and served on linguine—and seafood, beef, and pasta. Look for a daily breakfast buffet ($16) and a weekday pasta lunch buffet ($14). Also at the Delta is **The Dip** (summer daily 11:30 A.M.–11 P.M.), a poolside bar and grill where the views extend across the river and the menu extends from simple sandwiches to a surf and turf platter.

INFORMATION AND SERVICES
Tourist Information
The main **Visitor Information Centre** is right downtown, inside the lobby of City Hall

© ANDREW HEMPSTEAD

Start your exploration at City Hall, where you'll find the Visitor Information Centre.

(397 Queen St., 506/460-2129; mid-May– late June daily 8 A.M.–5 P.M., late June–Aug. daily 8 A.M.–8 P.M., Sept.–mid-Oct. daily 8 A.M.–5 P.M.). For advance information, contact **Fredericton Tourism** (506/460-2041 or 888/888-4768, www.tourismfredericton.ca).

Books and Bookstores
Stocking around 80,000 titles and newspapers from around the world, the downtown **Fredericton Public Library** (12 Carleton St., 506/460-2800; Mon.–Tues. and Thurs. 10 A.M.–5 P.M., Wed. and Fri. 10 A.M.–9 P.M.) has public Internet access.

Look no further than **Westminster Books** (445 King St., 506/454-1442) for local literature, including field guides and coffee table books. Around the corner, **Owl's Nest Bookstore** (390 Queen St., 506/458-5509) has a fantastic selection of used and out-of-print nonfiction.

Services
In an emergency, call 911 or the **RCMP** (1445 Regent St., 506/452-3400). For medical emergencies, contact the **Dr. Everett Chalmers Hospital** (Priestman St., 506/452-5400) or **Fredericton Medical Clinic** (1015 Regent St., 506/458-0200).

Hours at the **post office** (570 Queen St., 506/444-8602) are Monday–Friday 8 A.M.–5 P.M.; the retail outlets at Kings Place and the Fredericton Mall shopping centers have longer hours and are open Saturday.

Take your washing to **Spin & Grin** (516 Smythe St., 506/459-5552).

GETTING THERE
Fredericton Airport, 14 kilometers southeast of downtown off Highway 102, is served by daily **Air Canada** (506/458-8561 or 888/247-2262) flights from Montréal, Toronto, Ottawa, and Halifax. Avis, Hertz, Budget, and National have counters near the baggage carousels. Other airport facilities include a restaurant, a gift shop, free wireless Internet, and a business center. A cab to downtown costs $22.

Acadian (150 Woodside Ln., 506/458-6007) has daily bus service from Fredericton to Saint John, Moncton, and Edmundston. The small terminal is open daily 8 A.M.–8:30 P.M.

GETTING AROUND

Fredericton Transit (506/460-2200) has a web of nine bus routes connecting downtown with outlying areas (Mon.–Sat.). Fare is $2 per sector.

Look for cabs cruising downtown streets and waiting at major hotels, or call **Trius Taxi** (506/454-4444).

Car rental firms are plentiful. Chains in town include **Avis** (506/446-6006), **Budget** (506/452-1107), **Hertz** (506/446-9079), and **National** (506/453-1700).

Metered parking is plentiful in parking lots behind sights and curbside on Queen, King, upper York, Carleton, Regent, and Saint John Streets. The city provides free three-day parking passes for out-of-province visitors; the passes are available at City Hall and the Legislative Assembly building, both on Queen Street.

GAGETOWN AND VICINITY

The Saint John River downstream of Fredericton is dotted with islands, around which a skein of twisting channels is braided. It's beautiful countryside, and a delightful drive, with Gagetown, 40 kilometers from the capital, a good turnaround point.

The riverfront town of **Oromocto,** halfway to Gagetown, is built around Canadian Forces Base Gagetown, a military training installation located near the town center off Broad Road. The **CFB Gagetown Military Museum** (506/422-1304; July–Aug. Mon.–Fri. 8 A.M.–4 P.M. and Sat.–Sun. 10 A.M.–4 P.M., the rest of the year Mon.–Fri. noon–4 P.M.; free) has exhibits on the past and present of the Canadian armed forces since the late 18th century—weapons, uniforms, and other memorabilia.

From Oromocto, follow Highway 102 east along the river, cross divided Highway 2 (the TransCanada Highway), and you'll soon find yourself in the pretty riverfront town of Gagetown. Quite a bit goes on in this little town of 600 over the course of the season. Look for the four-day Queens County Fair (www.queenscountyfair.com) in mid-September, which features lots of agricultural attractions and competitions.

The **Queens County Museum** (69 Front St., 506/488-2966; June–mid-Sept. daily 10 A.M.–5 P.M.; $2) is in a handsome white wooden house that was the birthplace of Sir Leonard Tilley, one of the "Fathers of Confederation." The first floor is dutifully furnished with Loyalist antiques, and upstairs are vintage county exhibits.

Up the Saint John River

From Fredericton, Highway 2 (the TransCanada Highway) wends north along the Saint John River, crossing it numerous times before reaching Edmundston after 270 kilometers. As part of the transcontinental highway, it's easy smooth driving, but leave the main route and you'll find beautiful rural scenery and a region dotted with small towns. The region's highlights are within day-tripping distance of Fredericton, so you could travel as far as Hartland to see the world's longest covered bridge and then spend the afternoon at Kings Landing.

MACTAQUAC AND VICINITY

Stemming the flow of the Saint John River is **Mactaquac Dam,** part of a massive hydroelectric scheme 20 kilometers west of Fredericton. Completed in 1968, the dam rerouted the river and raised the water level 60 meters, flooding the valley and creating Mactaquac Lake Basin. Historic buildings from the flooded area found a new home at the Kings Landing Historical Settlement, a provincial heritage park that opened in 1974.

Mactaquac Generating Station (Hwy.

SAINT JOHN RIVER VALLEY

© ANDREW HEMPSTEAD

The Saint John River is a quiet waterway surrounded by pristine forest.

102, 506/462-3800; June–early Sept. daily 9 A.M.–4 P.M.; free), on the river's southern bank and just off the TransCanada Highway, offers guided tours. Below the dam, the **Mactaquac Visitor Interpretation Centre** (Hwy. 102, 506/363-3021; mid-May–Aug. daily 9 A.M.–4 P.M.; free) releases 300,000 salmon fry annually.

Mactaquac Provincial Park

Not all New Brunswickers were pleased with this massive river alteration, but the creation of 525-hectare Mactaquac Provincial Park, which opened the following year, was a sweetener. It's beside Highway 105 on the north side of the river, 24 kilometers upriver from Fredericton.

The setting's pièce de résistance is the 18-hole **Mactaquac Provincial Park Golf Course** (506/363-4926; greens fee $55), a challenging tree-lined layout considered one of Atlantic Canada's top public courses. The park also offers hiking trails, supervised beaches, bike rentals, picnic areas, and bass fishing. Park entry is $8 per vehicle per day.

The wooded campground has more than 300 sites ($25 unserviced, $28 with electrical hookups) with kitchen shelters, hot showers, a launderette, and a campers' store fronting the Mactaquac Lake Basin. The park and campground are open mid-May to mid-October and a day pass is $7 per vehicle.

◖ KINGS LANDING HISTORICAL SETTLEMENT

A marvelous counterpoint to Caraquet's Village Historique Acadien, this grand-scale living museum (Rte. 102, 506/363-4999; late May–mid-Oct. daily 10 A.M.–5 P.M.; adult $16, senior $14, child $11) is in a beautiful setting alongside the Saint John River, 35 kilometers west of Fredericton (take Exit 253 from Highway 2). The river valley was settled by Loyalists who arrived in New Brunswick in 1783, and it is this era through to the early 1900s that the village represents. Bring comfortable walking shoes, as the site spreads across 120 hectares with 70 houses and buildings—among them a sawmill, farmhouses, a school, a forge, and a printing office. Informative costumed "residents" depict rural New Brunswick life as it was lived in the 1800s. One of many interesting links to the past is an orchard where hybrid apples developed by Francis Peabody Sharp in the mid-1800s are grown. Demonstrations include horseshoeing, metal forging, cloth spinning and weaving, and farming. Special events include live theater, an Agricultural Fair in late August, the Provincial Town Criers' Competition in early September, and a Harvest Festival in early October to close out the season.

No one ever leaves the **Kings Head Inn** (506/363-4950; late May–mid-Oct. daily 11:30 A.M.–5 P.M.; lunches $7–14) complaining about being hungry. At the riverside end of the village, this restaurant serves up hearty fare like salmon chowder, crunchy almond fish cakes, and divine desserts that include maple-brandy squash pie.

TO GRAND FALLS

West from Kings Landing, the TransCanada Highway follows the Saint John River along one of its loveliest stretches. Tourism New Brunswick refers to this stretch of highway as the **River Valley Scenic Drive.** The Saint John is wide and blue, bounded by green fields and forests of maple and hemlock.

Woodstock

Just over 100 kilometers from Fredericton, Woodstock is an agricultural service center for this rich potato-producing region. The gracious 1884 red-brick courthouse is a dominant feature of the main street, but the **Colin's Log Cabin Diner** (539 Main St., 506/328-8553; daily 8 A.M.–8 P.M.; $8–17) is where you'll find the law-abiding locals. A cooked breakfast is $5, or double everything for a Giant Breakfast ($8).

◖ Hartland Covered Bridge

North from Woodstock, give the TransCanada Highway a miss and stick to Highway 103, which hugs the west bank of the Saint John River for 30 kilometers, from where it makes a sharp right turn and crosses the world's longest covered bridge before emerging in the village of Hartland. The bridge is only wide enough for one-way traffic, so make sure no one else is driving toward you before entering the bridge. Built in 1901, covered in 1921, and now protected as a national historic site, it stretches 391 meters over the Saint John River. On the east side is an information center (summer daily 9 A.M.–6 P.M.) with displays on the bridge's history and on other covered bridges in New Brunswick. From this point, a walking trail leads upstream and then along the Becaguimac Stream.

Grand Falls (Grand-Sault)

The otherwise placid Saint John River becomes a frothing white torrent when it plunges 23 meters over the stony cataract that gave Grand Falls, or Grand-Sault, its name. Below the falls, which have been harnessed to produce hydroelectric power, the tremendous force of the river has worn a two-kilometer-long,

horseshoe-shaped gorge through 70-meter-high rock walls. Here, the river is at its narrowest, and the gorge's bottleneck impedes the water's force. The river pushes through the narrows in tumultuous rapids, like pent-up champagne bursting from the bottle.

The **Malabeam Information Centre** (Madawaska Rd., 506/475-7769; early June–early Sept. daily 9 A.M.–6 P.M.; guided tour adult $8, child $5) makes a convenient starting point for exploring the area. From the center's rear windows, you'll see the thundering cataracts tumbling through the gorge. A two-kilometer-long path leads along the gorge to **La Rochelle.** From there, a rock staircase leads down to the cataract edge, where the agitated river swirls in the rocky wells. The river is most spectacular during spring runoff.

Several well-priced lodgings in Grand Falls make the town all the more appealing for overnight stays. The best choice is the **Quality Inn** (TransCanada Hwy., 506/473-1300 or 888/473-1300, www.choicehotels.ca; $110–160 s or d), on the north side of town. It has 100 rooms and cottages opposite an artificial pond, an indoor pool, a small fitness room, and a sauna.

EDMUNDSTON AND VICINITY

Originally settled by Acadian refugees on the site of a Malecite village, Edmundston boasts 17,000 residents, over 90 percent of whom are French speakers, a higher percentage than any other North American city outside Québec.

Sights and Recreation

For an insight into the area's checkered history and "mythical Madawaska," stop in at the **Madawaska Museum** (195 Blvd. Hébert, 506/737-5282; July–Aug. daily 9 A.M.–8 P.M., Sept.–June Wed.–Thurs. 7–10 P.M. and Sun. 1–5 P.M.; adult $4, child $2). But to truly experience the local Acadian-flavored culture, come for the five-day **Foire Brayonne** (506/739-6608, www.foirebrayonne.com), on the weekend closest to August 1. More than 100,000 people show up for the celebration of Brayon foods, music, dance, sports, and other entertainment.

SAINT JOHN RIVER VALLEY

Accommodations

Edmundston's ritziest lodging is the large **Clarion Hotel** (100 Rice St., 506/739-7321 or 800/576-4656, www.clarionhotel.com; from $125 s or d), which has spacious and elegantly decorated guest rooms, an indoor pool, a hot tub, a sauna, a restaurant, a lounge, and free wireless Internet throughout. With similar facilities is **Quality Inn Edmundston** (919 Canada Rd., 506/735-5525 or 800/563-2489, www.choicehotels.ca; $95–115 s or d). Both are accessed from Exit 18 of the TransCanada Highway.

Saint-Jacques

North of Edmundston, about halfway to the Québec border, is Saint-Jacques, home of **de la République Provincial Park,** where the highlight is the **New Brunswick Botanical Garden** (Exit 8 of the TransCanada Hwy., 506/737-5383; June–Sept. 9 A.M.–6 P.M., July–Aug. 9 A.M.–8 P.M.; adult $14, senior $12, child $7). If you've admired the flower-filled setting at the Montréal Botanical Garden, you will see a resemblance here. The formal garden complex on 17 hectares was designed by the same skilled Michel Marceau. It brims with 60,000 plants of 1,500 species. Roses, perennials, and rhododendrons bloom among the prolific posies in nine gardens, all orchestrated with classical music in a romantic vein. Other park facilities include an outdoor swimming pool, tennis courts, and a campground ($24–28).

Targeted at visitors entering New Brunswick from Québec, the **Provincial Visitor Information Centre** (506/735-2747; mid-May–early Oct. daily 10 A.M.–6 P.M., July–Aug. daily 8 A.M.–9 P.M.) is alongside the TransCanada Highway, nine kilometers south of the border.

Lac-Baker

Lac-Baker is in New Brunswick's remote northwestern corner, near where the Saint John River flows into the province from the northern reaches of Maine. Here you'll find all the quiet woodlands you could ever want, as well as the rustic **Camping RJ Belanger** (510 Church Rd., 506/992-2136; mid-May–mid-Sept.). The lakeshore complex lies several kilometers north of the river and has eight cabins ($75–95 s or d); campsites ($26–32); a dining room and canteen; and swimming, canoeing, and kayaking.

MOUNT CARLETON PROVINCIAL PARK

This remote 17,000-hectare park is a popular spot for hiking and wilderness camping. It is off Highway 385, 105 kilometers northeast of Perth-Andover (on the TransCanada Highway, halfway between Hartland and Grand Falls). If you're looping around the province between Campbellton and the Saint John River Valley via Highway 17, you can reach the park by following Highway 180 east from Saint Quentin to Highway 385. A day pass costs $8 per vehicle.

The park surrounds the Maritimes' highest point of land, **Mount Carleton** (820 meters). If you're keen on reaching the summit, wear sturdy shoes and bring a jacket to combat the winds. The easiest, marked ascent goes up a 4.4-kilometer trail through a spruce, fir, and yellow birch forest. The mountain's peak rises above the tree line and the view is marvelous, overlooking the adjacent mountains and lakes from a summit strewn with mountain cranberries and wild blueberries. Other trails in the 62-kilometer network include a 300-meter path to Williams Falls.

The park's main campground (506/235-6040; mid-May–mid-Sept.; $25) has 88 campsites, flush toilets, showers, kitchen shelters, a dump station for RVs, a playground, a boat-launching ramp, and swimming in Nictau Lake.

ACADIAN COAST

Along the eastern edge of New Brunswick is the Acadian Coast—a French-flavored realm of seaports, barrier beaches, sand dunes, salt marshes, sandy pine-clad shores, and rocky coastline. Northumberland Strait is the shallow, narrow sea strip between New Brunswick's southeastern coast and Prince Edward Island. Here the coastline attracts summertime sunbathers, swimmers, and windsurfers to welcoming beaches and waters warmed by the Gulf Stream. Farther north, the warm sea mixes with the cooler Gulf of St. Lawrence. Here the Labrador Current swirls in the open gulf, and the swift currents arrive ashore with low rolls of surf. Offshore, barrier islands hold sheltered seaports. Farthest north, the Baie des Chaleurs ("Bay of Warmth") is the shallow

sea pocket between northern New Brunswick and Québec's Gaspé Peninsula.

The essence of French-speaking Acadia is entwined in its dining and festivals. To understand the region's cultural roots, visit the Village Historique Acadien at Caraquet, where early Acadian life has been re-created with authentic buildings and costumed reenactors. In the south, Moncton, northern New Brunswick's trendy urban commercial and educational center, is Caraquet's bustling modern counterpoint—a very successful Acadia of the new millennium. Acadian pride runs high, and everywhere in the region the Acadian flag— the red, white, and blue French tricolor with a single gold star—is displayed prominently. But other ethnic groups are represented here as well, most notably the Irish.

HIGHLIGHTS

◖ Bore Park: OK, you don't *have* to visit Bore Park, but it's a good place to watch the tidal bore, and as it's home to the region's main information center, you can load up with brochures (page 61).

◖ Magnetic Hill: Magnetic Hill itself is mildly intriguing, but the surrounding commercial attractions – think zoo, water park, minigolf – make this a spot you'll want to take the family (page 63).

◖ Sackville Waterfowl Park: Birdwatchers will be enthralled with the many and varied bird species that call this reserve home (page 68).

◖ Parlee Beach: Buff – and not so buff – bods flock to Parlee Beach for its long expanse of sand, warm swimming water, and holiday vibe (page 70).

◖ Le Pays de la Sagouine: The literary world learned about Acadian life from the novels of Antonine Maillet, and this energetic historic park in her hometown brings the writing to life (page 71).

◖ Lamèque International Baroque Music Festival: Even if, like me, you're not an aficionado of early music, the remote setting and the haunting sounds of this musical extravaganza will stay with you (page 77).

◖ Village Historique Acadien: Experience Acadian life up close and personal at this outdoor museum (page 78).

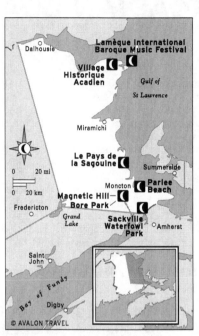

LOOK FOR ◖ TO FIND RECOMMENDED SIGHTS, ACTIVITIES, DINING, AND LODGING.

Stretched-out distances notwithstanding, getting around is easy and very manageable. Highway 11 lopes along most of the three coasts from seaport to seaport, with the sea almost always within view. End to end, it's an easygoing 10-hour one-way drive between Campbellton and Shediac, if you take your time. But by all means, take the side roads branching off the main route and amble even closer to the water to explore the seaports and scenery. For example, Highway 11 diverges from the coast and cuts an uninteresting beeline between Miramichi and Bouctouche.

Coastal Highway 117 is far more scenic, running through Kouchibouguac National Park and curling out to remote Point Escuminac—a lofty shale plateau at Miramichi Bay's southeastern tip, frequented, in season, by thousands of migratory seabirds.

PLANNING YOUR TIME

Moncton, at the south end of the Acadian Coast, is central to the entire Maritimes region, so you'll probably pass through at least once on your Atlantic Canada vacation. The bustling downtown core is well worth exploring,

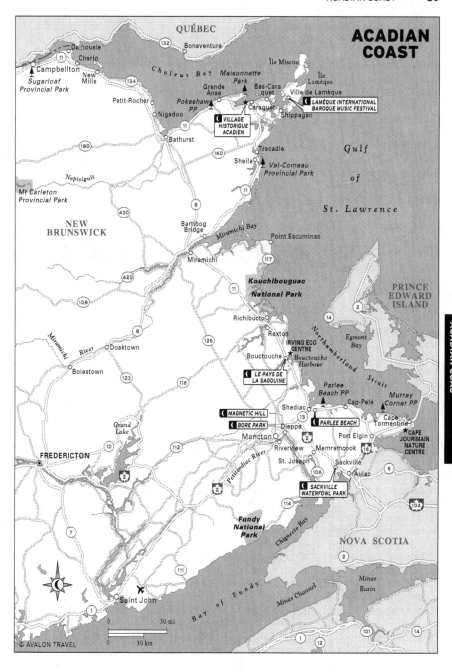

ACADIAN COAST

QUÉBEC

Bonaventure

Dalhousie
Charlo
Campbellton
Sugarloaf Provincial Park
New Mills
Petit-Rocher
Nigadoo
Chaleur Bay *Maisonnette Park*
Grande Anse
Pokeshaw PP
Bathurst
Caraquet
Shippagan
Île Miscou
Île Lamèque
Ville de Lamèque
Bas-Caraquet
LAMÈQUE INTERNATIONAL BAROQUE MUSIC FESTIVAL

VILLAGE HISTORIQUE ACADIEN

Tracadie
Sheila
Val-Comeau Provincial Park

Gulf

of

St. Lawrence

Nepisiguit
Mt Carleton Provincial Park

NEW BRUNSWICK

Bartibog Bridge
Miramichi Bay
Miramichi
Point Escuminac

Kouchibouguac National Park

PRINCE EDWARD ISLAND

Richibucto
Rexton
IRVING ECO CENTRE
Bouctouche
Bouctouche Harbour
LE PAYS DE LA SAGOUINE

Egmont Bay

Doaktown
Miramichi River
Boiestown

Northumberland Strait

Parlee Beach PP
Cap-Pelé
Murray Corner PP
Cape Tormentine
CAPE JOURIMAIN NATURE CENTRE

MAGNETIC HILL
BORE PARK
Shediac
PARLEE BEACH
Grand Lake

Dieppe
Moncton
Riverview
St. Joseph
Memramcook
Port Elgin
Sackville
Aulac
FREDERICTON
Petitcodiac River

SACKVILLE WATERFOWL PARK

Fundy National Park

Chignecto Bay

NOVA SCOTIA

Saint John

Bay of Fundy
Minas Channel
Minas Basin

0   30 mi
0   30 km

© AVALON TRAVEL

with **Bore Park** a good starting point. If you're traveling with children, they'll definitely want you to stop at the city's **Magnetic Hill** commercial attractions. Getting back to nature, a nearby highlight for bird-watchers is **Sackville Waterfowl Park.**

If you look at a map of New Brunswick, you'll see that the Acadian Coast extends the entire length of the province (it's 320 kilometers from Moncton to Campbellton), so to avoid returning along the coastal highway, plan on combining time along the Acadian Coast with the drive down the Saint John River Valley to Fredericton—in effect, two of three legs of a loop around the entire province.

This circuit will take four days at an absolute minimum, and preferably six. If the weather is warm, factor in some beach time, and there's no better place for this than **Parlee Beach,** just a short drive from Moncton. As you drive north, it is impossible not to be intrigued by the pockets of Acadian culture. The best place to learn more about this culture's tragic history and revitalized present are **Le Pays de la Sagouine** and **Village Historique Acadien.** The final highlight of the Acadian Coast is the **Lamèque International Baroque Music Festival,** and if you're anywhere near the region in late July, I encourage you to attend this unique event.

Moncton

With a population of 64,000 (128,000 in Greater Moncton), this bustling city is the geographic center of the Maritimes. It does an admirable job of promoting its many and varied attractions, and it exudes a vitality and energy unlike that anywhere else in the province. Visitors can take in two very different natural attractions—one related to the colossal Fundy tides, the other to a quirk of nature—while children will be attracted to Atlantic Canada's largest theme park. The bustling downtown core is packed with well-priced accommodations, good restaurants, and a lively nightlife.

Moncton lies 155 kilometers northeast along the Fundy Coast from Saint John and 175 kilometers east from the capital, Fredericton. It's also centrally located to other provinces, with the Nova Scotia border 37 kilometers southeast and the Confederation Bridge to Prince Edward Island 92 kilometers to the east.

The city is officially bilingual. About 30 percent of the population speaks French as a first language. So while most everyone also speaks English, knowledge of French will help the visitor.

History
The site of modern-day Moncton was along a

Mi'kmaq portage between the Bay of Fundy and Northumberland Strait, but the first permanent settlers were Acadians, who arrived in the 1740s. The British captured nearby Fort Beauséjour in 1755 and deported the Acadians in 1758. The area was settled by Germans soon after, but it wasn't until the 1840s, when shipbuilding became a major business, that the town began its real growth. Moncton began its first real boom when the Intercolonial Railway chugged into New Brunswick and designated the town as the railroad's Atlantic hub. By 1885, the city was an industrial center with a tannery, a soap factory, a cotton mill, a brassworks, a sugar refinery, foundries, lumberyards, and riverside wharves.

Moncton has maintained its economic edge through the decades, and the wealth has spilled over into the suburbs of Dieppe and Riverview. Riverview keeps a low profile. Dieppe is another story. After World War II, returning soldiers renamed the town, formerly Leger Corner, to honor their fallen comrades who died on the beaches at Dieppe, France. The suburb now rivals Moncton in economic importance and is the site of the airport, Atlantic Canada's largest amusement center, and one of the region's largest shopping malls.

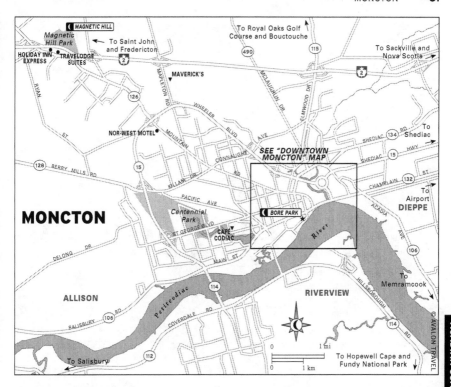

DOWNTOWN SIGHTS

Downtown Moncton is centered on the north side of "The Bend," a sharp turn in the Petitcodiac River. The busy and bustling **Main Street,** a block in from the river, has brick sidewalks, old-time lampposts, and park benches beneath sapling trees. The following sights are ordered by distance from the water, starting at the riverfront and moving outward. There's no parking on Main Street. Instead, use one of the adjacent side streets and deposit a loonie ($1 coin) for an hour in a metered parking slot, or park in one of the nearby lots.

(Bore Park

The huge Bay of Fundy tides reach Moncton twice daily, when a tidal bore, a lead wave up to 60 centimeters high, pulses up the Petitcodiac River. Within an hour or so, the muddy bed of the Petitcodiac—locally dubbed the "Chocolate River"—will be drowned under some 7.5 meters of water. The tourist information center on Main Street can provide a tidal schedule. While the Moncton tourism folks put watching the tidal bore on their list of must-see attractions, many locals call it the Total Bore. In any case, the sight is most impressive at those times of the month when the tides are highest—around the full and new moons.

The best place to witness the tidal phenomenon is off Main Street at Bore Park, which is dotted with shade trees and park benches. This is also the site of the main tourist information center (where you can find out what time the tidal bore will arrive) and the start of a riverside boardwalk.

Moncton Museum

Artifacts from the city's history—from the age of the Mi'kmaq to World War II—and touring

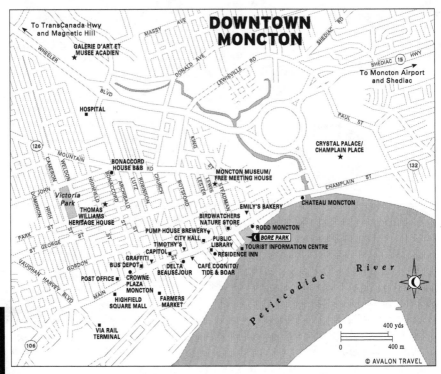

national exhibits are displayed at the former city hall (20 Mountain Rd., 506/856-4383; Mon.–Sat. 9 A.M.–4:30 P.M. and Sun. 1–5 P.M.; donation). When the building was modernized, the city architect concocted an interesting arrangement that combined the building's original native sandstone facade with an updated interior.

Adjacent to the Moncton Museum, the tidy, small **Free Meeting House** (Moncton's oldest building) dates to 1821 and served as a sanctuary for religious groups as diverse as Anglicans, Adventists, Jews, and Christian Scientists. If you're interested in seeing the interior, ask at the museum.

Thomas Williams Heritage House

A century ago, the Intercolonial Railroad brought the movers and shakers to town. Among them was Thomas Williams, the railroad's former treasurer. His 12-room Second Empire–style mansion (103 Park St., 506/857-0590; mid-June–late Aug. Tues.–Sun. 10:30 A.M.–4:30 P.M.; donation) was built in 1883 and is now open to the public. Elegantly furnished with period pieces, it's a showpiece of the good old days. The Verandah Tea Room serves tea, coffee, and muffins in summer.

Galerie d'Art et Musée Acadien

The Acadian region is as creatively avant-garde as it is historic. At the Université de Moncton, in the Clément Cormier Building, this gallery and museum (off Wheeler Blvd., 506/858-4088; June–Sept. Mon.–Fri. 10 A.M.–5 P.M., Sat.–Sun. 1–5 P.M.; $2) touch upon numerous aspects of Acadian culture in the combined exhibits. The university itself spreads across a large campus north of downtown. It is Atlantic Canada's sole French-speaking university and

ANDREW HEMPSTEAD

Moncton's history is evident in the architecture.

grants degrees in business, fine arts, science, education, nursing, and law.

◖ MAGNETIC HILL

If you've got children, Magnetic Hill will be the focus of your time in Moncton. To get there from downtown, follow Mountain Road northwest; from the TransCanada Highway, take Exit 488. The namesake Magnetic Hill (506/853-3540; mid-May–early Sept. daily 8 A.M.–8 P.M.; $3 per vehicle) is just a hill, but if you believe your eyes, you'll agree it's one of the world's oddest. Is Magnetic Hill magnetic? It must be. The unassuming dirt road, which seems to defy the rules of logic, is said to be Canada's third most popular natural tourist attraction, behind Niagara Falls and the Canadian Rockies.

The hill's slope plays tricks on anything with wheels. Set your car at the hill's "bottom," shift into neutral, and release the brake. The car appears to coast backward *up* the hill. Cars aren't the only things that defy gravity here. A stream alongside the road seems to flow uphill, too.

The illusion baffled Monctonians for decades. Before the 1900s, the local farmers fought the incline when they tried to haul wagons "down" the hill. Several decades later, reporters from Saint John discovered Magnetic Hill. Their newspaper coverage of the "natural phenomenon" brought a slew of spectators, and the stream of nonbelievers hasn't stopped since.

If you think a strange and otherworldly force powers Magnetic Hill, think again. For the record, the whole countryside hereabouts is tilted. Magnetic Hill forms the southern flank of 150-meter-high Lutes Mountain northwest of Moncton. The hill is an optical illusion, and believe it or not, the hill's top crest is lower than the hill's "bottom." Try to walk the hill with your eyes closed. Your other senses will tell you that you are traveling down rather than up.

Commercial Attractions

So many tourists arrived to observe the illogical hill that an adjacent gift shop was opened in the 1970s, and the area quickly grew into a concentration of family-oriented attractions.

Magnetic Hill Zoo (125 Magnetic Mountain Rd., 506/877-7718; mid-June–early Sept. daily 9 A.M.–8 P.M.; adult $12.50, senior $11.50, child $9) bills itself as the largest zoo in Atlantic Canada. It houses some 100 animal species, including zebras, reindeer, tigers, camels, wolves, and gibbons. A petting zoo entertains the wee ones and the crowds gather daily at 2:30 P.M. for Meet the Ranger.

Magic Mountain Water Park (506/857-9283; mid-June–mid-Aug. daily 10 A.M.–7 P.M., mid-Aug.–early Sept. daily 10 A.M.–6 P.M.; $25.50 for those over 48 inches tall and $19.50 for those under) has an outdoor wave pool, numerous chutes, tube rides, and mini-golf. (No, the water here does not run uphill.)

The Boardwalk (506/852-9406; summer daily 9 A.M.–dusk) offers go-kart rides, mini-golf, batting cages, a driving range, and a playground. **Wharf Village** (506/858-8841) is a shopping area featuring arts and crafts and a family-style restaurant overlooking an artificial pond.

ACADIAN COAST

RECREATION
Centennial Park
At the western side of town, this 180-hectare spread of greenery (St. George Blvd., 506/853-3516; daily 9 A.M.–11 P.M.) makes a pleasant place to picnic and relax amid woodlands and offers hiking trails and a lake with a sandy beach. Summer activities include lawn bowling, swimming, tennis, and canoeing and paddling on the lake. In winter, lighted trails invite cross-country skiers, skaters, and hockey players to take to the frozen lake.

Fun Parks
The area has sprouted other amusements besides those at Magnetic Hill. A short, narrow river tributary separates Moncton from adjacent Dieppe, where **Crystal Palace** (499 Paul St., Dieppe, 506/859-4386; Mon.–Fri. noon–8 P.M., Sat.–Sun. 10 A.M.–8 P.M.) rises from the far side of the Highway 15 rotary. This complex is an architectural wonder, a geodesic dome of angled glass walls with the Crystal Palace Amusement Park (adult $22, child $18; unlimited rides) and a science center within. **Champlain Place,** Atlantic Canada's largest one-level shopping mall, is next door.

ENTERTAINMENT AND EVENTS
Theater
In the mid-1990s, the **Capitol** (811 Main St., 506/856-4379) was transformed from a dowdy downtown movie theater to a gracious symbol of the past. Today, this lovely old grande dame, ornately decorated with frescoes and murals, glitters with concerts, ballets, shows, and film festivals. Check www.capitol.nb.ca for a schedule.

Bars and Nightclubs
Most of the drinking and dancing action happens along Main Street, where the college crowds gather at bars and nightclubs and tables spill onto the streets. The **Pump House Brewery** (5 Orange Ln., 506/855-2337) is a little quieter than most and has a sun-drenched patio out front. It brews its own beer, which is available on draught and in bottles. For a quiet drink, **Le Galion,** in Château Moncton (100 Main St., 506/870-4444) is a good choice. With seating inside and out, you get to enjoy the river scenery up close and can sip a beer while waiting for the tidal bore in a bright, contemporary setting. In the Crowne Plaza Moncton, **Bin 1005 Wine Bar** (1005 Main St., 506/854-6340) is a typical upscale hotel lounge, with the bonus of an excellent wine list.

Oxygen (125 Westmorland St., 506/854-0265) is generally regarded as one of the province's hottest destinations for dance parties, with DJs spinning discs on weekends.

Festivals and Events
One of the city's most-loved gatherings is the mid-August **Atlantic Seafood Festival** (506/855-8525, www.atlanticseafoodfestival.com), hosted by venues as varied as hotel dining rooms and outdoor dining areas along the main street. As the name suggests, the emphasis is on local seafood. You can watch oyster-shucking demonstrations, cheer on your favorites in various cooking competitions, and take part in the street party.

Moncton hosts the **World Wine & Food Festival** (506/532-5333, www.wineexpo.ca) over the first week of November. It brings together wine representatives from around the world with celebrity chefs, but the ambience is anything but pompous as the general public gathers to soak up the worldly atmosphere.

The mid-November **Festival International du Cinéma Francophone en Acadie** (506/855-6050, www.ficfa.com) is a major French-language film festival.

SHOPPING
Major shopping malls in the area include Dieppe's **Champlain Place** (corner of Paul St. and Champlain St.) and **Moncton Mall** (1380 Mountain Rd., 506/858-1380), but to sample the local flair for arts and crafts, you'll need to look elsewhere. Artisans market wares at the downtown **Moncton Market** (Westmorland St., www.marchemonctonmarket.ca, Sat. 7 A.M.–1 P.M.). **Gifts Galore** (569 Main St.,

506/857-9179) carries a little bit of everything—glass, pottery, pewter, T-shirts, and more. It helps to speak French at some shops, such as **Galerie Sans Nom** (Aberdeen Cultural Centre, 140 Botsford St., 506/854-5381), a cooperative where the emphasis is on contemporary arts and crafts.

ACCOMMODATIONS AND CAMPING

Lodgings are conveniently concentrated in two main areas—downtown and at the city's northwestern corner, near Magnetic Hill. Overall, prices are reasonable, especially for the larger downtown properties.

$50-100

Bonaccord House Bed and Breakfast (250 Bonaccord St., 506/388-1535; $60 s, $80 d) is a charming meld of Victoriana, with four guest rooms and wireless Internet, a balcony, and a veranda, located in a tree-shaded residential area. Breakfast is included, and you can walk to downtown in 10 minutes.

$100-150

The five-story **Rodd Moncton** (434 Main St., 506/382-1664 or 800/565-7633, www.roddvacations.com; $125 s or d, extra for river views) overlooks Bore Park with 97 guest rooms and an outdoor pool. The rooms aren't particularly large, but the location still makes this place a good value, especially considering breakfast is included.

On the eastern edge of downtown, **Château Moncton** (100 Main St., 506/870-4444 or 800/576-4040, www.chateaumoncton. ca; $130–180 s or d) is a distinctive red-roofed chateau-style lodging overlooking the tidal bore. Guests enjoy 97 modern and spacious rooms and suites with wireless Internet access, an exercise room, voice mail, free local calls, and daily newspapers. The hotel also has a riverside deck and a pleasant lounge.

The motels clustered around Magnetic Mountain (take Exit 488 from the TransCanada Highway) are mostly within this price range. **Holiday Inn Express** (2515 Mountain Rd., 506/384-1050 or 800/465-4329, www.hie-moncton.com; $125 s or d) has the most facilities, with an indoor pool, restaurant, lounge, hot tub, sauna, business center, and family suites with bunk beds.

The folks at **Nor-West Motel** (1325 Mountain Rd., 506/384-1222 or 800/561-7904, www.norwestmotel.com; $105 s or d) have done a great job of upgrading an older motel out near Magnetic Hill, with colorful flower arrangements out front adding to the appeal. A hot breakfast is included in the rates.

Travelodge Suites (2475 Mountain Rd., 506/852-7000 or 800/525-4055, www.travelodge.com; from $145 s or d) has 77 spacious, nicely appointed guest rooms with free in-room movies, work desks, and small fridges. A daily newspaper, wireless Internet access, and a hot buffet breakfast are included in the rates.

$150-200

My pick for downtown accommodations is the ◖ **Residence Inn** (600 Main St., 506/854-7100 or 888/236-2427, www.marriott.com; from $159 s or d), with 133 modern and spacious guest rooms in the heart of the city. Many units have one or two bedrooms, and all have kitchens. Other amenities include an indoor pool, a fitness room, and a family-style steakhouse.

Crowne Plaza Moncton (1005 Main St., 506/854-6340 or 877/227-6963, www.cp-moncton.com; $189 s or d) comes complete with contemporary decor, the best beds in town, wireless Internet access, CD clock radios, and many other niceties. The top floor is a restaurant and lounge. Other amenities include an indoor pool, a fitness room, an affordable steakhouse, and a wine bar.

Delta Beauséjour (750 Main St., 506/854-4344 or 888/890-3222, www.deltahotels.com; from $189 s or d) is equal to the Crowne Plaza in style, service, and facilities, but everything is a little less new. On the plus side, the 310 guest rooms are very spacious. Other facilities include a café, two restaurants, a lounge, and an indoor pool.

Ramada Palace Hotel (499 Paul St., Dieppe, 506/858-8584 or 800/561-7108, www. crystalpalacehotel.com; $180–280 s or d) is part of the Crystal Palace amusement park, which makes it the perfect place for families looking for a break from New Brunswick's natural and historic wonders. Most of the 115 guest rooms are fairly standard, but the themed fantasy suites—one employs a rock-and-roll theme complete with a replica of a 1959 pink Cadillac for a bed—are the highlight for those willing to pay extra. Other amenities include an indoor pool, a restaurant (with a great Sunday brunch), and a lounge.

Campground

Shediac, 20 kilometers northeast of Moncton, is covered in the *Strait Coast* section, but the beachside campground within **◖ Parlee Beach Provincial Park** (506/533-3363; $32) makes a great alternative to city camping—although it does get busy. The turnoff is on the east side of Shediac. Amenities include hot showers, a playground, and over 165 sites.

FOOD

You might stumble on a few Acadian dishes, but most local restaurants keep it simple and straightforward, appealing to the college crowd with cheap food and energetic service.

Cafés

Main Street is the place to head for a coffee at a street-side table, and no one pours better drinks than **Timothy's World Coffee** (735 Main St., 506/854-7210; Mon.–Fri. 7 A.M.–10 P.M., Sat. 9 A.M.–10 P.M.).

In a red-brick heritage building across the road from Timothy's, **Café Cognito** (700 Main St., 506/854-4888; Mon.–Fri. 7:30 A.M.– 5:30 P.M., Sat. 10 A.M.–4 P.M.) also has excellent coffee, along with chai lattes and sandwiches made to order.

Once you have your sandwich to go from Café Cognito, plan on a picnic in Bore Park, but also pick up a sweet treat from **◖ Emily's Bakery** (34 King St., 506/857-0966; Mon.

9 A.M.–4 P.M., Tues.–Fri. 9 A.M.–5:30 P.M., Sat. 9 A.M.–4:30 P.M.).

Although it's away from downtown, to the northwest toward Magnetic Hill, **Café Codiac** (666 St. George Blvd., 506/854-7100; Mon.– Fri. 7 A.M.–6 P.M., Sat. 8 A.M.–6 P.M.; lunches $5.50–8) is worth searching out for excellent coffee, delicious soups made daily, and a wide range of baked goodies.

Restaurants

Most of the pubs along Main Street serve food, but the offerings at **Tide and Boar** (700 Main St., 506/857-9118; daily for lunch and dinner; $12–25) are a notch above the rest. The platters to share are a good way to start, before moving on to a smoked trout salad or pizza with caramelized plums and goat cheese. Wash your meal down with a beer from the long list of choices or a house-made ginger beer and rum.

Pump House Brewery (5 Orange Ln., 506/855-2337; daily from 11:30 A.M.; $9–18) has been around since the late 1990s, and it remains popular both for its handcrafted beer and well-priced food. Highlights are the wood-fired pizzas, including such varieties as roast vegetable and bacon cheeseburger.

Stylish **◖ Maverick's** (Future Inns, 40 Lady Ada Blvd., 506/855-3346; Mon.–Thurs. 6:30 A.M.–10 P.M., Fri. 6:30 A.M.–11 P.M., Sat. 7:30 A.M.–11 P.M., Sun. 7:30 A.M.–10 P.M.; $18– 35) is out on the main highway through town. A lunchtime carvery buffet is just $15, and specials (available most days) include a $30 meal for two on Tuesday evenings. All the favorites are offered—an extra-thick cut of prime rib, tender rib eye, and a variety of strip loins—and they all come exactly how you ordered them. The menu also offers top-notch seafood, including boiled lobster. A well-rounded wine list adds to the appeal.

At the west end of the main street, **Graffiti** (897 Main St., 506/382-4299; Mon.–Sat. 11 A.M.–11 P.M., Sun. 4–11 P.M.; $11–18) is a cheery little Mediterranean restaurant filling two floors of a narrow historic building. The orange walls are decorated with large pieces of interesting art and tables are well spaced across tiled floors. The menu takes from a variety of Mediterranean countries—think vegetarian couscous and pizzas on pita bread, with a few seafood and steak dishes topping out the inexpensive menu.

At the same end of town as Graffiti, **T-bones** (Crowne Plaza Moncton, 1005 Main St., 506/854-6340; daily 6 A.M.–2 P.M. and 5–10 P.M.; $17–39) has a predictable wide-ranging menu that doesn't offend anyone, with choices that include everything from vegetarian fettuccine to 16-ounce namesake T-bone steaks.

Magnetic Hill Dining

Overlooking the pond at Wharf Village is **Wharf Village Restaurant** (506/859-1812; May–Oct. daily 10 A.M.–8 P.M.; lunches $7–13), which does a fine job feeding theme park visitors familiar family fare at good value for the dollar. Seating is outside on a covered deck or inside with basic decor and air conditioning. On the right side of the restaurant is a self-service counter hawking soup and sandwiches to go.

INFORMATION AND SERVICES
Tourist Information

The city's main **Tourist Information Centre** (506/853-3590 or 800/363-4558, www. gomoncton.com; mid-May–early Sept. daily 8:30 A.M.–5:30 P.M.) is on the east side of downtown in Bore Park.

Books and Bookstores

Moncton Public Library is at Blue Cross Centre (644 Main St., 506/869-6000; summer Mon. and Fri. 9 A.M.–5 P.M. and Tues.–Thurs. 9 A.M.–8:30 P.M., the rest of the year Mon. and Fri.–Sat. 9 A.M.–5 P.M., Tues.–Thurs. 9 A.M.–8:30 P.M.). If you're looking for French-language reading material, **Librairie Acadienne** has it at the Université de Moncton's Taillon Building (Archibald St., 506/858-4140).

The city's largest bookstore is **Chapters** (499 Paul St., Dieppe, 506/855-8075), east of downtown in the Champlain Place complex.

Also here is the smaller **Coles** bookstore (506/854-7397).

Services

Moncton Hospital is on the road between downtown and Magnetic Hill (135 MacBeath Ave., 506/857-5111). **Hôpital Dr. Georges L. Dumont** is the French hospital (330 University Ave., 506/862-4000). For the **RCMP,** call 911 or 506/857-2400.

For postal services, go to the main **post office** (281 St. George St. at Highfield St.). The VIA Rail terminal behind Highfield Square on Main Street has **storage lockers,** as does the Acadian bus terminal (961 Main St.). **St. George Laundromat** (66 St. George Blvd.) is open daily 8:30 A.M.–9 P.M.

GETTING THERE
Air

Greater Moncton Airport is 10 kilometers from downtown Moncton on Champlain Street/Highway 132 (a continuation of Main Street in Moncton) in adjacent Dieppe. The airport has a food court, a lounge, wireless Internet, and car rental desks (Avis, Budget, Hertz, and National). A metered taxi ride with **Air Cab** (506/857-2000) to Main Street in Moncton costs about $18 one-way.

The airport is served by **Air Canada** (888/247-2262) from Halifax, Montréal, and Toronto and by **WestJet** (800/538-5696) from Toronto, Hamilton, and Calgary.

Train and Bus

Moncton is served by **VIA Rail** (506/857-9830 or 800/561-3952) on its route between Montréal and Halifax. The terminal is behind Highfield Square on Main Street.

By virtue of its central location, Moncton is a hub for **Acadian** buses (961 Main St., 506/859-5060). Services run to Saint John, Fredericton, Charlottetown, Halifax, and along the Acadian Coast to Campbellton.

GETTING AROUND

Codiac Transit (506/857-2008) operates local bus service (Mon.–Wed.

ACADIAN COAS

and Sat. 6:20 A.M.–7 P.M., Thurs.–Fri. 6:20 A.M.–10:15 P.M.).

Air Cab (506/857-2000) charges $2.85 to start and about $1.20 per kilometer.

Major car rental companies with downtown and airport desks are **Avis** (506/855-7212), **Budget** (506/857-3993), **Hertz** (506/858-8525), and **National** (506/382-6114).

Southeast from Moncton

Geologically, the area southeast of Moncton is related to the Bay of Fundy, but as it is separated from the rest of the Fundy Coast, it is covered here. Unless you choose to stop at the attractions detailed below, you'll cross over to Nova Scotia in a little over 30 minutes and be in Halifax in three hours.

MEMRAMCOOK
Take Highway 106 southeast from Moncton for 20 kilometers to reach the village of Memramcook and **Monument-Lefebvre National Historic Site** (488 Centrale St., 506/758-9808; June–mid-Oct. daily 9 A.M.–5 P.M.; adult $4, senior $3.50, child $2), which is dedicated to the memory of Father Camille Lefebvre, founder of Canada's first French-language university. Within the historic Monument-Lefebvre building on the Memramcook Institute campus, the **Acadian Odyssey** exhibit explains Acadian survival with a series of displays.

SACKVILLE
The 17th-century settlers who founded Sackville, 45 kilometers southeast of Moncton, emigrated from around the estuaries of western France, so they were experienced in wresting tidelands from the sea. By creating an extensive system of dikes called *aboideaux,* they reclaimed thousands of acres of Chignecto Isthmus marsh and brought the extremely fertile alluvial lands into agricultural production. Their raised dikes can be seen around Sackville and into Nova Scotia.

Mount Allison Academy (later University) was founded here in 1843; a "Female Branch" was opened 11 years later. In 1875, the university gained the distinction of being the first in the British Empire to grant a college degree to a woman.

The beautiful campus is still at the heart of this town, surrounded by stately houses and tree-shaded streets. A number of artists have chosen Sackville as their home, and one of the best places to see their work is at Mount Allison University's **Owens Art Gallery** (61 York St., 506/364-2574; Mon.–Fri. 10 A.M.–5 P.M., Sat.–Sun. 1–5 P.M.; free). The Owens ranks as one of the major galleries in the province and emphasizes avant-garde work by local, regional, and national artists.

◖ Sackville Waterfowl Park
If you're short on time and can stop at only one of the area's several wildlife sanctuaries, make it the Sackville Waterfowl Park, a 22-hectare reserve where more than 170 bird species have been recorded. The main entrance, just a few blocks north of downtown, is easy to miss but offers interesting park displays. From this point, the sanctuary (open daily dawn to dusk) spreads out, with trails routed through bush and bleached wooden walkways crossing wetlands. Ducks, herons, teals, and bitterns are common, while spotting loons, Canada geese, sandpipers, and peregrine falcons is possible.

Accommodations and Food
For a place to stay, consider ◖ **Marshlands Inn** (55 Bridge St., 506/536-0170, www.marshlands.nb.ca; $105–125 s or d), among the province's best-value lodgings. The inn, built in the 1850s, got its name from an early owner, who christened the mansion in honor of the adjacent Tantramar Marshes. The resplendent white wooden heritage inn sits back

© ANDREW HEMPSTEAD

Boardwalks provide easy access to Sackville Waterfowl Park.

from the road under shady trees and offers 20 guest rooms furnished with antiques and a dining room of local renown. Open daily for guests and nonguests, the dining room is smart and elegant, with many steak and seafood choices ($17–30), as well as a dish of seafood crepes filled with lobster, shrimp, and scallops ($24).

SACKVILLE TO AULAC

Another prime birding site is not far from Sackville. From Dorchester, 14 kilometers west of Sackville on Highway 106, turn off on Highway 935. The backcountry gravel road loops south around the **Dorchester Peninsula**—the digit of land separating Shepody Bay from the Cumberland Basin.

Some 50,000 semipalmated sandpipers nest from mid-July to mid-September between Johnson Mills and Upper Rockport, where the road loops back toward Sackville. Roosting sites lie along pebble beaches and mudflats, and the birds are most lively at feeding time (low tide). Smaller flocks of dunlins, white-rumped

sandpipers, and sanderlings inhabit the area from late September to October.

Across the Chignecto Isthmus is an incredibly fertile habitat so rich in waterfowl and birds that the early Acadian settlers described the area as a *tintamarre* ("ceaseless din"), now known as **Tantramar Marshes.** A few roads haphazardly thread through the marshes, and there's no official approach to bird-watching here. Head off the TransCanada Highway anywhere and wander; you can't go wrong on any of the backcountry roads from the Sackville area to the province's border crossing.

AULAC AND VICINITY

The last town before crossing into Nova Scotia is Aulac, on the Bay of Fundy side of the TransCanada Highway at the turnoff to the Confederation Bridge.

Fort Beauséjour

Eight kilometers east of Sackville, a signpost marks the turnoff from the TransCanada Highway to the Fort Beauséjour National Historic Site (111 Fort Beauséjour Rd., 506/364-5080; June–mid-Oct. daily 9 A.M.–5 P.M.; adult $4, senior $3.50, child $2), overlooking the Cumberland Basin just west of the Nova Scotia border. Continue on the road to the fort ruins, which mark France's last-ditch military struggle against the British, who threatened Acadia centuries ago. France lost the fort in 1755 after a two-week siege. The Brits renamed it Fort Cumberland and used it in 1776 to repel an attack by American revolutionaries. The fort stood ready for action in the War of 1812, though no enemy appeared. Fort Cumberland was abandoned in the 1830s, and nature soon reclaimed the site. Some of the ruins have since been restored. Facilities include a picnic area and a museum–visitor center with exhibits on life in the old days.

Tintamarre Sanctuary

Tintamarre National Wildlife Area fans out beyond the fort ruins. Continue on Highway 16 for about 10 kilometers to Jolicure, a village at the reserve's edge. No trails penetrate

ACADIAN COAST

the 1,990-hectare mix of marshes, uplands, old fields, forests, and lakes. A few dikes provide steady ground through some of the terrain, but you are asked to stay on the roads encircling the area to do your bird-watching. Amid the cattails, sedges, and bulrushes, sightings include migratory mallards, grebes, red-winged blackbirds, yellow warblers, swamp swallows, common snipes, black ducks, Virginia rails, and bitterns; short-eared owls take wing at dusk. Bring binoculars—and insect repellent. The area is thick with mosquitoes.

Strait Coast

The Strait Coast runs from Cape Tormentine, New Brunswick's easternmost extremity, to Miramichi, 143 kilometers northeast of Moncton. It fronts Northumberland Strait, the narrow body of water separating New Brunswick from Prince Edward Island, and so it's no surprise that the main towns and attractions are focused on the water.

CAPE TORMENTINE TO SHEDIAC

Most travelers drive, literally, over the top of Cape Tormentine on their way to Prince Edward Island via the **Confederation Bridge.**

Cape Jourimain Nature Centre

Nestled below the southern end of the Confederation Bridge, this interpretive center (5039 Hwy. 16, 506/538-2220; mid-May–mid-Oct. daily 9 A.M.–5 P.M., until 7 P.M. in July and August; donation) sits at the gateway to a 675-hectare national wildlife area, home to a reported 170 species of birds. The center has varying ecology exhibits, is the starting point for an 11-kilometer trail system, and has a restaurant.

The nearest camping is at **Murray Beach Provincial Park** (Hwy. 955, 506/538-2628; May–Sept.; $24–28), 13 kilometers west toward Shediac. In addition to a good swimming beach, amenities include more than 100 campsites on a wooded bluff, showers, a laundry, and a playground.

Continuing West

A few fine quiet beaches dot the **Cap-Pelé**

area, farther west on Highway 15. At Gagnon Beach, **Camping Gagnon Beach** (506/577-2519 or 800/658-2828, www.campinggagnon.com; late May–mid-Sept.; $26–32) has 208 sites with full hookups plus a separate wooded tenting area.

SHEDIAC

The self-proclaimed "Lobster Capital of the World," 20 kilometers northeast of Moncton, Shediac backs up its claim with the **world's largest lobster**—an 11-meter-long, cast-iron sculpture by Winston Bronnum sitting beside the road into town. For the real stuff, head for the town's restaurants, which have a reputation for some of the province's best lobster dinners.

◖ Parlee Beach

The little town can be crowded on weekends—this is *the* beach getaway for Moncton residents. **Parlee Beach Provincial Park** (506/533-3363) protects one of many beaches strung out to the east. This placid three-kilometer-long beach is popular for the warmth of the water, which reaches 24°C in summer. The entrance is from the eastern edge of Shediac, along an access road that ends at a massive parking lot behind low sand dunes. Behind the beach are changing rooms, a café, and a restaurant, while down on the beach swimming is supervised. Access is $11 per vehicle per day (collected in summer only).

Accommodations and Camping

The beautiful white **Auberge Belcourt Inn** (310 Main St., 506/532-6098 or 877/466-

8496, www.innthyme.com; $115–150 s, $125–165 d) was built in 1911 for a Shediac dentist, but it has been thoroughly modernized, with contemporary guest rooms and amenities like wireless Internet. The inn sits back from the road beneath stately trees. It's near the western edge of town, just a quick stroll from the beach.

In the heart of Shediac, **(Tait House** (293 Main St., 506/532-4233 or 888/532-4233, www.maisontaithouse.com; from $159 s or d) is a beautifully restored 1911 mansion with historic guest rooms complemented by contemporary features, such as polished hardwood floors and plush mattresses topped with white linens. The in-house restaurant offers a menu of local ingredients prepared with cooking styles from throughout Europe.

Parlee Beach Provincial Park (Hwy. 133, 506/533-3363; $33) is within walking distance of the beach. It has hot showers, a playground, and more than 165 sites. Reservations are not accepted, so plan to arrive around lunchtime to secure a spot.

Food

Near the end of the road out to Point-de-Chêne Marina (turn off the highway on the east side of town), you find **(Captain Dan's** (506/533-2855; daily 11 A.M.–10 P.M.; $12–27), a super-casual, perennially crowded bar and grill with a beachin' atmosphere and great food. Hang loose, watch the boats, and feel your blood pressure drop.

BOUTOUCHE

North of Shediac, Highway 11 zips through a wooded corridor, sacrificing scenery for efficiency. For a taste of the slower pace of rural coastal Acadia, strike out on any of the local highways (such as 530, 475, or 505) to the east, which hug the coast and lead to quiet beaches at Saint-Thomas, Saint-Edouard-de-Kent, and Cap-Lumière. Along the way, the routes come together at Bouctouche, 30 kilometers north of Shediac. You can learn about two centuries of Acadian culture at **Le Musée de Kent** (150 Chemin du Couvent, 506/743-5005;

Le Musée de Kent is a good place to learn about Acadian history.

July–early Sept. Mon.–Sat. 9 A.M.–5:30 P.M., Sun. noon–6 P.M.; adult $3, senior $2, child $1), in a restored 1880 convent two kilometers east of downtown, but the two main local attractions are Le Pays de la Sagouine and Irving Eco-Centre.

(Le Pays de la Sagouine

Author Antonine Maillet is renowned in the literary world for her colorful descriptions of Acadian life, and so there is no better place to re-create the ambience of her work than this lively outdoor theme park in her hometown of Bouctouche. Le Pays de la Sagouine (57 Acadie St., 506/743-1400; late June–early Sept. daily 10 A.M.–4:30 P.M.; adult $17, senior $15, child $10) is on a peninsula and islet with a hamlet of houses and other buildings, a reception center, and a crafts shop. The highly recommended guided tour (included in admission) leaves daily at 11 A.M. and 3 P.M. Evening dinner theater (in French) is the site's big draw; you'll have a choice of seafood, Canadian, or—the best bet—traditional Acadian fare. And your meal will be accompanied by Acadian music, which might be in any number of styles. The show only is adult $44, child $22, or pay $72 and $47 respectively for park admission, dinner, and show.

Irving Eco-Centre

Continue through town beyond Le Musée de Kent and turn north up the coast to reach Irving Eco-Centre (Hwy. 475, 506/743-2600), which preserves the ecosystem surrounding a 12-kilometer-long sand dune along Bouctouche Bay. The ecosystem was created as a public relations gesture by New Brunswick megacorporation J. D. Irving Ltd. (petroleum, logging, you name it). A two-kilometer-long wheelchair-accessible boardwalk leads from an interpretive center through the dunes. Other trails traverse forest and marshland. Naturalists work on-site May–November, doing ecology research and leading school field trips and such. Bird-watchers will spot great blue herons, piping plovers, and long-winged terns, among other species.

KOUCHIBOUGUAC NATIONAL PARK

The Northumberland Strait coast ends at Kouchibouguac National Park (506/876-2443), a 238-square-kilometer gem of a park that takes its name from the Mi'kmaq word for "river of the long tides"—a reference to the waterway that meanders through the midsection of the low-lying park. Some pronounce it "KOOSH-ee-buh-gwack," others say "kee-gee-boo-QUACK," Parks Canada says it's "kou-she-boo-gwack," and you'll hear many other variations.

Slender barrier islands and white beaches and dunes, laced with marram grass and false heather, face the gulf along a 25-kilometer front. A gray seal colony occupies one of the offshore islands. In the park's interior, boardwalks ribbon the mudflats, freshwater marshes, and bogs, and nature trails probe the woodlands and fields.

Park Entry

Entry fees are charged mid-May to mid-

Kouchibouguac National Park

October. A one-day pass is adult $8, senior $7, child $4 (to a maximum of $20 per vehicle).

Recreation

The land and coast are environmentally sensitive; park officials prefer that you stay on the trails and boardwalks or use a bike to get around on the 30 kilometers of biking and hiking trails. Naturalist-led programs and outings are organized throughout summer. Check at the Visitor Reception Centre and campgrounds for a schedule.

Trails that explore the park's varied ecosystems include the short **Kelly's Beach Boardwalk,** the **Pines** and **Salt Marsh** trails, and the 1.8-kilometer **Bog** trail. You can take longer hikes on the **Clair-Fontaine** (3.4 kilometers), **Osprey** (5.1 kilometers), and **Kouchibouguac** (14 kilometers; allow five hours) trails.

The Black, St. Louis, Kouchibouguac, and other rivers that weave through the park are wonderful to explore by canoe, kayak, rowboat, or pedalboat. Those watercraft, as well as fishing equipment and bicycles, are available at **Ryan's Rental Centre** (506/876-3733; mid-June–early Sept. daily 8 A.M.–9 P.M.). Fishing in the national park also requires a license: $10 per day or $35 for an annual license. **Swimming** is supervised at Kelly's Beach in summer; swimming at Callander's and other beaches is unsupervised.

Camping

Within the park are two campgrounds. Finding a site shouldn't be a problem, except in July and August. At these times, reservations through the **Parks Canada Campground Reservation Service** (905/426-4648 or 877/737-3783, www.pccamping.ca) are wise. The cost is $11 per booking plus the campsite fee.

South Kouchibouguac Campground (mid-May–mid-Oct.; $28–33) offers 265 unserviced sites and 46 sites with power hookups. Civilized comforts include showers, flush toilets, kitchen shelters, firewood ($7 per bundle), launderettes, and a campers' store near the beach.

Côte-à-Fabien Campground (mid-June–early Sept.; $14) has 32 primitive campsites but few facilities and no hookups.

Information

Make your first stop the **Visitor Reception Centre** (1 km inside the main entrance off Hwy. 134, 506/876-2443, www.pc.gc.ca; mid-May–mid-June and early Sept.–mid-Oct. daily 9 A.M.–5 P.M., mid-June–early Sept. daily 8 A.M.–8 P.M.). For a memorable introduction, be sure to see the 20-minute slide presentation, *Kouchibouguac,* which takes the viewer on a seasonal trip through the park's sublime beauty and changing moods. Campsite registration is handled at the center, and information on activities, outdoor presentations, and evening programs is posted here, too.

Miramichi River

The gorgeous Miramichi (meer-ma-SHEE) River and its myriad tributaries drain much of the interior of eastern New Brunswick. The river enjoys a wide reputation as one of the best (if not *the* best) Atlantic salmon waters in the world. In the early 17th century, Nicolas Denys, visiting the Miramichi estuary, wrote of the salmon, saying: "So large a quantity of them enters into this river that at night one is unable to sleep, so great is the noise they make in falling upon the water after having thrown or darted themselves into the air."

Leaving the conurbation of Miramichi near the river's mouth, Highway 8 follows the river valley southwest for most of its length. Most of the valley is lightly populated.

MIRAMICHI

Don't get too confused if that old road map of New Brunswick you're using doesn't seem to jibe with the signs you're seeing out the

© ANDREW HEMPSTEAD

Miramichi skyline

car window. No, the cities of Chatham and Newcastle didn't disappear; in 1995 they amalgamated into a single municipal entity called Miramichi. The former Chatham is now Miramichi East, and the former Newcastle is Miramichi West.

Old French maps of this area show the Miramichi River as the Rivière des Barques, the "River of Ships." From as early as the last quarter of the 18th century, the locally abundant timber and the deepwater estuary made this an excellent location for the shipbuilding industry. The Cunard brothers began their lucrative shipbuilding empire at Chatham in 1826 and built some of the finest vessels of their day. The industry thrived for half a century and then faltered and faded, leaving no physical evidence—outside of museums—that it ever existed.

Sights

At Miramichi East (Chatham), before Highway 11 crosses to the north side of the river, **St. Michael's Basilica** (10 Howard St., 506/778-5150; daily 8 A.M.–4 P.M.; free) is a distinctive sandstone church overlooking the river.

Across the river, **Rankin House Museum** (2224 King George Hwy., 506/773-3448; July–Aug. Mon.–Fri. 9 A.M.–5 P.M.; free) has a surprisingly large collection of memorabilia amassed from throughout northeastern New Brunswick. Ask here for a brochure detailing buildings of historical interest within walking distance of the museum.

Farther southwest along Highway 8 is **Miramichi West** (formerly Newcastle), a pleasant river town with lots of old buildings that center on a small square hosting a memorial to Lord Beaverbrook. One of the most powerful newspapermen in British history, he was raised at what is now known as **Beaverbrook House** (518 King George Hwy., 506/624-5474; June–Aug. Mon.–Fri. 9 A.M.–5 P.M., Sat. 10 A.M.–5 P.M.), now a small museum dedicated to his life and links to New Brunswick. If you're traveling with children, head down to **Ritchie Wharf,** an old shipbuilding center that has been converted to a playground.

Festivals and Events

In the mid-19th century, Middle Island, a river island just east of town, was the destination of thousands of Irish emigrants, many of them fleeing the catastrophic potato famine of the 1840s. Their descendants are still in the region, and since 1984 the area has celebrated its Irish heritage with **Canada's Irish Festival** (506/778-8810, www.canadasirish-fest.com). The three-day event in mid-July includes concerts, dances, a parade, lectures and music workshops, booths selling Irish mementos and books, and the consumption of a good deal of beer.

The first week of August is the **Miramichi Folksong Festival** (www.miramichifolksong-festival.com), which opens with an outdoor gospel concert and continues with a shindig of traditional and contemporary singing, dancing, and fiddling.

Accommodations and Camping

Step back in time at the **Governor's Mansion Inn** (62 St. Patrick's Dr., Nelson, 506/622-3036 or 877/647-2642, www.governorsmansion.ca; $69–109 s or d), which is made up of two historic homes in a quiet out-of-town setting across the road from the Miramichi River. Some rooms share bathrooms while the largest have private four-piece bathrooms, separate sitting areas, and river views.

At the upper end of the price range is the **Rodd Miramichi River** (1809 Water St., Miramichi East, 506/773-3111 or 800/565-7633, www.roddvacations.com; $125–165 s or d), a modern riverside complex where rooms are painted in warm heritage colors. Amenities include a restaurant and indoor pool.

Enclosure Campground (10 km south of town along Hwy. 8, 506/622-8638; $28–32) has 100 campsites, hiking trails, a beach, a heated pool and spa, kitchen shelters, a canteen, and a playground.

Food

Angler's Reel (Rodd Miramichi River, 1809 Water St., Miramichi East, 506/773-3111; $14–26), on the south side of the river, has a dependable breakfast, lunch, and dinner menu, but to eat with the locals, head to the nearby **Old Town Diner** (1724 Water St., 506/773-7817; daily 7 A.M.–7 P.M.; $8–12), where a cooked breakfast with all the coffee you can drink is just $6.

Information

Miramichi Visitor Centre (199 King St., 506/778-8444; June–Aug. daily 10 A.M.–5 P.M.)

SALMON FISHING ON THE MIRAMICHI

Fly-fishing is the only method allowed for taking Atlantic salmon. Fish in the 13- to 18-kilogram range are not unusual; occasionally, anglers land specimens weighing up to 22 kilograms. The salmon season runs from mid-May to mid-October. Nonresidents are required to hire guides, who are plentiful hereabouts.

Riverside fishing resorts, which let you drop a line in rustic elegance, are a popular way to enjoy the piscatorial experience. They're not cheap, however. One of the best and most historic is **Upper Oxbow Outdoor Adventures** (near Trout Brook, 506/622-8834 or 888/227-6100, www.upperoxbow.com), which has been in operation since 1823 and through five generations of the same family. The company offers day trips ($190 per person, guides and equipment included), but most anglers stay overnight on packages that typically cost from $300 per person per day, including meals, accommodation, and guiding.

A more luxurious option is **Pond's Resort** (Porter Cove Rd., Sillikers, 506/369-2612 or 877/971-7663, www.pondsresort.com), which charges $400-450 per person per day for lodging, meals, and guided fishing.

is beside Highway 11 as it enters town from the south.

MIRAMICHI TO FREDERICTON

From Miramichi, it's 180 kilometers south along the Miramichi River to Fredericton, the capital of New Brunswick. The route is a handy highway if you're planning to drive a loop around the province, but aside from the rural scenery, the biggest draw to the drive is salmon fishing.

Doaktown

Crossing through the deep interior of the province, Highway 8 runs alongside the famed salmon-rich Miramichi River to Doaktown, 86 kilometers southwest of Miramichi. Squire Robert Doak from Scotland founded the town and gave it a boom start with gristmills and paper mills in the early 1800s. The squire's white wooden house (with some original furnishings) and nearby barn have been set aside as **Doak Provincial Historic Site** (386 Main St., 506/365-2026; late June–early Sept. Mon.–Sat. 9:30 A.M.–4:30 P.M., Sun. 1–4:30 P.M.; donation).

Also in town, the **Atlantic Salmon Museum** (263 Main St., 506/365-7787; June–Aug. daily 9 A.M.–5 P.M., Sept.–Oct. Mon.–Sat. 9:30 A.M.–4 P.M.; adult $5, senior $4, child $3) will be especially interesting to anglers. Exhibits depict the life cycle and habitat of this king of game fish, as well as the history of the art of catching it (including a collection of rods, reels, and gaudily attractive flies). Live salmon specimens at various stages of development swim in the aquariums.

Boiestown

Another well-conceived museum is the **Central New Brunswick Woodmen's Museum** (Hwy. 8, 506/369-7214; June–early Oct. daily 9 A.M.–5 P.M.; adult $6, senior $5, child $3), which spreads over 15 acres along Highway 8 near Boiestown. The museum's exhibits explain forestry's past and present. Among the buildings are replicas of a sawmill, a blacksmith shop, a wheelwright shop, a trapper's cabin, a bunkhouse, and a cookhouse. A Forestry Hall of Fame remembers the Paul Bunyans of New Brunswick's timber industry, and a miniature train makes a 15-minute loop through the grounds.

Baie des Chaleurs

North of Miramichi Bay, the Acadian peninsula juts northeast into the Gulf of St. Lawrence. One side of the peninsula faces the Gulf of St. Lawrence, while the other side fronts the Baie des Chaleurs. In contrast to the wild Gulf of St. Lawrence, the shallower Baie des Chaleurs is warm and calm. Busy seaports dot the eastern coast of the bay—the region's commercial fishing fleets lie anchored at Bas-Caraquet, Caraquet, and Grande-Anse. Interspersed between the picturesque harbors are equally beautiful peninsulas, coves, and beaches. Swimming is especially pleasant along the sheltered beaches, where the shallow sea heats up to bathtub warmth in summer. Across the bay, Québec's Gaspé Peninsula is usually visible, sometimes with startling clarity when conditions are right. From Bathurst west, the fishing villages give way to industrial towns.

ACADIAN PENINSULA
Bartibog Bridge

It's a 20-minute drive on Highway 11 from Miramichi to this bayside town, where **MacDonald Farm Historic Site** (600 Hwy. 11, 506/778-6085; late June–early Sept. daily 9:30 A.M.–4:30 P.M.; adult $3, senior $2, child $1.50) re-creates a Scottish settler's life in 1784. Guides take visitors through the two-story stone farmhouse, fields, orchards, and outbuildings.

Val-Comeau Provincial Park

Farther north on Highway 11, Val-Comeau

Provincial Park comprises lush sphagnum bogs, formed when the last ice sheet melted and pooled without a place to drain on the flat terrain. Seabirds inhabit the nutrient-rich marshes; the park is known for bird-watching, and there is an observation tower for good views. Val-Comeau also offers a campground (506/393-7150; June–mid-Sept.; $25–32), with 55 sites, swimming areas, and a playground.

Shippagan

New Brunswick's largest commercial fishing fleet is based in this sheltered bay at the tip of the Acadian Peninsula, 100 kilometers northeast of Miramichi. The **Aquarium and Marine Centre** (100 Aquarium St., 506/336-3013; June–late Sept. daily 10 A.M.–6 P.M.; adult $8.50, senior and child $6.50) opens up the world of gulf fishing with exhibits and viewing and touch tanks holding 125 native fish species.

Camping Shippagan (4 km west of town, 506/336-3960; June–Sept.; $20–28) enjoys a great location, right on the water with a nice beach. Amenities include firewood, showers and washrooms, a licensed restaurant, kitchen shelters, a picnic area, a launderette, and organized activities.

ÎLE LAMÈQUE

Offshore of Shippagan, Île Lamèque noses into the gulf at the brow of the Acadian Peninsula. Connected to the mainland by a bridge, the island changes with the seasons: Spring brings a splendid show of wildflowers; summer brings wild blueberries ripening on the barrens; autumn transforms the landscape to a burnished red. The spruce trees here are bent and dwarfed by the relentless sea winds, but oysters, moon snails, blue mussels, and jackknife clams thrive along the beautiful white sandy beaches.

◖ Lamèque International Baroque Music Festival

Île Lamèque is best known for this late July festival (506/344-5846 or 877/377-8003, www.festivalbaroque.com), as unlikely as that

ACADIAN DEPORTATION

After the signing of the Treaty of Utrecht in 1713, England had demanded but not enforced an oath of allegiance from the Acadians who lived under its jurisdiction. By the 1750s, however, the British decided to demand loyalty. Those who refused to sign the oath of allegiance were rounded up and deported, and their villages and farmlands were burned.

The Acadians being deported were herded onto ships bound for the English colonies on the Eastern seaboard or any place that would accept them. Some ships docked in England, others in France, and others in France's colonies in the Caribbean. As the ports wearied of the human cargo, many of them refused the vessels entry, and the ships returned to the high seas to search for other ports willing to accept the Acadians.

In one of the period's few favorable events, the Spanish government offered the refugees free land in Louisiana, and many settled there in 1784, where they became known as Cajuns. Many Acadians fought the British in guerrilla warfare or fled to the hinterlands of Cape Breton Island, Prince Edward Island, New Brunswick, and Québec.

Exact deportation numbers are unknown. Historians speculate that 10,000 French inhabitants lived in Acadia in 1755; by the time the deportation had run its course in 1816, only 25 percent of them remained. The poet Longfellow distilled the tragedy in his *Evangeline,* a fictional story of two lovers divided by the events.

ACADIAN COAS

may seem out here among the peat bogs and fishing villages. It is the only festival in North America dedicated to the celebration of music from the baroque period (1600–1760) and has been attracting the world's best early music performers since the early 1970s. The setting is superb—almost divine—within the acoustically perfect 1913 Church Sainte-Cecile.

Accommodations and Camping

The fanciest digs on the island are at **Auberge des Compagnons** (11 rue Principale, Lamèque, 506/344-7766 or 866/344-7762, www.aubergedescompagnons.ca; $115–190), a modern 16-room lodge with sweeping water views. The restaurant serves a buffet-style breakfast, which is extra.

Campers should continue across the bridge to Île Miscou, a blissfully remote island barely touched by the modern world. **Plage Miscou** (22 Allée Alphonse, 506/344-1015; mid-May–Sept.; tents $21, hookups $32) is a simple campground with limited facilities but a pleasant bay outlook.

CARAQUET

From the south, Highway 11 lopes into town and turns into a boulevard lined with shops, lodgings, and sights. Established in 1758, picturesque Caraquet (pop. 4,200), 32 kilometers northwest of Shippagan, is northern New Brunswick's oldest French settlement and is known as Acadia's cultural heart.

Sights and Recreation

◖ VILLAGE HISTORIQUE ACADIEN

Ten kilometers west of Caraquet, Village Historique Acadien (14311 Rte. 11, Rivière du Nord, 506/726-2600; mid-June–late Sept. daily 10 A.M.–6 P.M.; adult $16, senior $14, child $11) provides a sensory journey through early Acadia. To re-create the period from 1780 to 1890, more than 40 rustic houses and other authentic buildings were transported to this 1,133-hectare site and restored. The buildings—including a church, a smithy, farmhouses, a school, a printing shop, a carpenter's shop, a gristmill, and others—are spread across woods and fields along the North River. You walk the dusty lanes or hop aboard a horse-drawn wagon to get from one building to the next, where costumed "residents" describe their daily lives, their jobs, and surroundings in French and English. Out in the park, two "post houses" serve sandwiches, snacks, and drinks. The site also holds **La Table des Ancêtres,**

which serves typical Acadian dishes at reasonable prices.

THE ACADIAN MUSEUM

The Acadian Museum (15 St-Pierre Blvd., 506/726-2682; June–mid-Sept. Mon.–Sat. 10 A.M.–6 P.M., Sun. 1–6 P.M.; adult $3, child $1) is a less ambitious look at local history than Village Historique Acadien, but it's still a worthwhile stop. The adjacent Carrefour de la Mer (51 St-Pierre Blvd., 506/726-2688), whose name translates to "Crossroads of the Sea," encompasses the local information center, mini-golf, a playground, and a restaurant.

FISHING

Caraquet's fishing fleet is based at **Bas-Caraquet,** a 10-minute drive east on Highway 145 toward Île Lamèque.

Festivals and Events

The town is the place to be for early August's two-week **Festival Acadien** (www.festivalacadien.ca), one of the province's best-attended events. It includes the blessing of the huge fishing fleet by the local Roman Catholic clergy; jazz, pop, and classical music concerts; live theater; food and drink; and the Tintamarre, a massive street celebration on Acadia Day (August 15).

Accommodations and Food

The distinctive three-story, crisply colored red-and-green ◖ **Hotel Paulin** (134 St-Pierre Blvd., 506/727-9981 or 866/727-9981, www.hotelpaulin.com; $195–315 s or d) is a family-run boutique hotel that has been entertaining guests since 1901. The 12 guest rooms have hardwood floors, comfortable beds, and a low-key but stylish decor. The top floor Waterfront Suites are huge. The downstairs restaurant oozes charm and opens nightly for creative table d'hôte dining.

GRANDE-ANSE

Highway 11 continues to the coast, where it takes a turn west to Grande-Anse. For a swim in the warm bay, take Highway 320, the narrow road that diverges to the right, to **Maisonnette Park,** an exquisite spread of beach overlooking Caraquet across Baie Caraquet. The warmwater beach is a favorite, especially when the tide retreats to reveal sand dune fingers washed by shallow, sun-heated waters. Seabirds are everywhere: You'll see them in large numbers on nearby aptly named Bird Island, where the long bluffs at **Pokeshaw Community Park** overlook rookeries of squawking cormorants.

In town, **Musée des Papes** (140 Acadie St., 506/732-3003; mid-June–Sept. daily 10 A.M.–5 P.M.; adult $5, senior and child $2.50) commemorates the visit of Pope John Paul II to New Brunswick in 1985. Exhibits include vestments, chalices, and other ecclesiastical paraphernalia, plus a detailed scale replica of St. Peter's Basilica.

BATHURST AND VICINITY

The town of Bathurst (pop. 12,000) sits by its own fine natural harbor at the vertex of Nepisiguit Bay, a broad gulf on the Baie des Chaleurs. It's 75 kilometers west of Caraquet, or 60 kilometers north of Miramichi as you shoot up Highway 8.

Daly Point Wildlife Reserve spreads across 40 hectares of salt marshes, woodlands, and fields northeast of town; an observation tower provides views of nesting ospreys, various seabirds, and songbirds. To get there, take Bridge Street (the Acadian Coastal Drive) east from Bathurst, then turn left on Carron Drive. Bring insect repellent.

Bathurst to Campbellton

Highway 11 stays inland for the scenically dull 85-kilometer stretch between Bathurst and Charlo. Far preferable is coastal Highway 134, which runs through the fishing villages of Nigadoo, Petit-Rocher, Pointe-Verte, and Jacquet River. The coast between Bathurst and Dalhousie is famed for sightings of a phantom ship. Numerous witnesses over the years have described a ship under full sail engulfed in flames on the bay; sometimes the vision includes a crew frantically scurrying across the deck. Some say the vision dates from the Battle

of Restigouche (1760)—the last naval engagement between France and England in this part of eastern Canada—when France's fleet was destroyed by the British.

La Fine Grobe Sur-Mer (289 Main St., Nigadoo, 506/783-3138; daily 5–10 P.M.; $15–31) enjoys a delightful setting on the beach, separated from the main road by a small but lovely wood. Georges Frachon has been cooking up delightful meals here since 1973. You can order French-inspired dishes like chateaubriand, herb-crusted rack of lamb, and seafood pancakes.

Farther northwest, in New Mills, the **Auberge Blue Heron** (Hwy. 134, 506/237-5560; May–Oct.; $79–140 s or d) has seven guest rooms furnished with antiques. Set back from the road in an oversized former farmhouse opposite Heron Island, it's a setting worthy of provincial heritage inn status.

Eel River Bar, south of Dalhousie, is one of the world's longest sandbars. With freshwater on one side and saltwater on the other, it's a popular spot for beach-walking and swimming.

CAMPBELLTON

At the head of the Baie des Chaleurs, the New Brunswick and Gaspé coastlines meet near Campbellton (pop. 7,400), the area's largest town. A bridge here spans the broad mouth of the Restigouche River to connect with Québec's Highway 132. Highway 17 plunges deep into the unpopulated interior of New Brunswick, across the Restigouche Uplands. Along this route, it's 92 kilometers to Saint-Quentin, where you can veer east to Mt. Carleton Provincial Park or continue another 80 kilometers to join the Saint John River valley at Saint-Léonard.

Sights and Recreation

Galerie Restigouche (39 Andrew St., 506/753-5750; adult $2) is a public art gallery displaying works by local, national, and international artists, as well as natural history and science exhibits.

Sugarloaf Provincial Park (Exit 415 of Hwy. 11, 506/789-2366) overlooks the whole region. A year-round chairlift offers views to the 305-meter gumdrop-shaped peak of Sugarloaf Mountain. The park also has hiking trails, chairlift-assisted mountain biking, tennis courts, and supervised swimming. In winter, the park is popular for snowmobiling, skating, and cross-country skiing. The park campground is open mid-May–mid-October and has 76 wooded sites for $25–33.

Accommodations and Food

Campbellton's most interesting accommodation is also the least expensive. **HI-Campbellton** (1 Ritchie St., 506/759-7044, www.hihostels.ca; mid-June–Aug.) is in an old lighthouse along the Restigouche River. It has 20 beds in dormitories, a small kitchen, and a common area. Members of Hostelling International pay $24 per night and nonmembers pay $28.

The centrally located **Super 8** (26 Duke St., 506/753-7606 or 877/582-7666, www.super8campbellton.com; $115–145 s or d) has an indoor swimming pool and complimentary breakfast.

www.moon.com

DESTINATIONS | ACTIVITIES | BLOGS | MAPS | BOOKS

MOON.COM is ready to help plan your next trip! Filled with fresh trip ideas and strategies, author interviews, informative travel blogs, a detailed map library, and descriptions of all the Moon guidebooks, Moon.com is all you need to get out and explore the world—or even places in your own backyard. While at Moon.com, sign up for our monthly e-newsletter for updates on new releases, travel tips, and expert advice from our on-the-go Moon authors. As always, when you travel with Moon, expect an experience that is uncommon and truly unique.

KEEP UP WITH MOON ON FACEBOOK AND TWITTER
JOIN THE MOON PHOTO GROUP ON FLICKR

MAP SYMBOLS

▦ Expressway	◖	Highlight	✈	Airfield	♟	Golf Course
Primary Road	○	City/Town	✈	Airport	▯	Parking Area
Secondary Road	◉	State Capital	▲	Mountain	▰	Archaeological Site
Unpaved Road	⊛	National Capital	✦	Unique Natural Feature	⚲	Church
Trail	★	Point of Interest			▮	Gas Station
Ferry	•	Accommodation	⏧	Waterfall	▱	Glacier
Railroad	▼	Restaurant/Bar	▲	Park		Mangrove
Pedestrian Walkway	▪	Other Location	⬯	Trailhead		Reef
Stairs	⋀	Campground	⤧	Skiing Area		Swamp

CONVERSION TABLES

°C = (°F − 32) / 1.8
°F = (°C x 1.8) + 32
1 inch = 2.54 centimeters (cm)
1 foot = 0.304 meters (m)
1 yard = 0.914 meters
1 mile = 1.6093 kilometers (km)
1 km = 0.6214 miles
1 fathom = 1.8288 m
1 chain = 20.1168 m
1 furlong = 201.168 m
1 acre = 0.4047 hectares
1 sq km = 100 hectares
1 sq mile = 2.59 square km
1 ounce = 28.35 grams
1 pound = 0.4536 kilograms
1 short ton = 0.90718 metric ton
1 short ton = 2,000 pounds
1 long ton = 1.016 metric tons
1 long ton = 2,240 pounds
1 metric ton = 1,000 kilograms
1 quart = 0.94635 liters
1 US gallon = 3.7854 liters
1 Imperial gallon = 4.5459 liters
1 nautical mile = 1.852 km

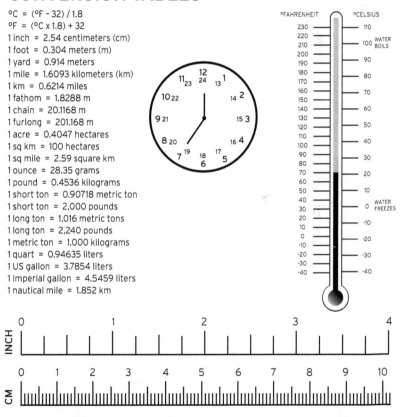

MOON SPOTLIGHT NEW BRUNSWICK
Avalon Travel
a member of the Perseus Books Group
1700 Fourth Street
Berkeley, CA 94710, USA
www.moon.com

Editor: Jamie Andrade
Series Manager: Kathryn Ettinger
Copy Editor: Teresa Elsey
Graphics and Production Coordinator:
   Lucie Ericksen
Cover Designer: Kathryn Osgood
Map Editor: Albert Angulo
Cartographers: Chris Hendrick, Chris Markiewicz,
   Kat Bennett, June Thammasnong

ISBN-13: 978-1-61238-157-2

Text © 2012 by Andrew Hempstead.
Maps © 2012 by Avalon Travel.
All rights reserved.

Some photos and illustrations are used by permission
and are the property of the original copyright
owners.

Front cover photo: blue and green water on the
   Atlantic Coast, New Brunswick © Donald Fink/
   Dreamstime.com

Title page photo: lighthouse on the eastern coast of
   New Brunswick © Ed Corey/123RF

Printed in the United States

ABOUT THE AUTHOR

Andrew Hempstead

© DIANNE MELTON

On his first trip to Atlantic Canada, Andrew Hempstead made a beeline for the coast to photograph the legendary Nova Scotia sunrise. He then headed to the nearest local restaurant, and wearily ordered the daily breakfast special without bothering to check what it was: cod fried in pork fat, pickled beets, and a side of baked beans.

With this traditional (and unexpected) introduction to Canada's east coast, Andrew set off on a road trip that stretched the term "unlimited mileage" on his rental car to the limit. Teaming up with knowledgeable local Ted Vautour for part of the trip, Andrew traveled to the farthest corners of all four provinces.

Andrew has been writing since the late 1980s, when, after leaving a career in advertising, he took off for Alaska, linking up with veteran travel writer Deke Castleman to help research and update the fourth edition of the Moon Handbook to Alaska and the Yukon. He has authored guidebooks to the Maritimes, Newfoundland and Labrador, Alberta, British Columbia, the Canadian Rockies, Vancouver and Victoria, and Western Canada, as well as contributing to guidebooks on the San Juan Islands and the Pacific Northwest. He has also worked on multiple guidebooks to New Zealand and Australia.

Andrew lives with his wife Dianne, daughter Brio, and son Macsen in Banff, Alberta. When not working on his books, Andrew spends as much time as possible enjoying the wonderful surroundings in which he lives: hiking, fishing, golfing, camping, and skiing.